Stolen Sisters

* * *

Stolen Sisters

The Story of Two Missing Girls, Their Families and
How Canada Has Failed Indigenous Women

*
* *
*

Emmanuelle Walter

Translated by Susan Ouriou and Christelle Morelli

Foreword by Melina Laboucan-Massimo

HarperCollins Publishers Ltd

To adolescence.
For Maisy and Shannon, wherever they may be.

Grandfather said you don't want to understand someone if you are stealing, or have stolen, all their property.
It might make you feel bad about what you did if you understood them.

—Jim Harrison, *Dalva*

This issue is not a women's issue, this is not an Aboriginal issue. This is a human tragedy, and this is a national disgrace.

—Dawn Harvard, interim president of the Native Women's Association of Canada, in a speech given on Parliament Hill, October 4, 2013

CONTENTS

Stolen Sisters

* * *

Entering the village of Kitigan Zibi from the south.

FOREWORD

The day I learned that my sister Bella had been found dead on the terrace of a high-rise condo near Toronto's waterfront, with no explanation of why or how she fell, was the day I understood what it feels like to grieve so deeply and so immensely that nothing else matters. It felt like there was no end to the screaming sadness.

When I am asked what Missing and Murdered Indigenous Women (MMIW) means to me, I think of pain, grief, shock, sadness and anger. I think of the gaping void that families suffer after experiencing the loss of cherished and loved ones in such drastic, traumatic and violent ways that no woman or girl should ever be subjected to. I think of the ripple effects that families experience after a tragic event like this happens, and how a family struggles to cope with this trauma. I think of the younger generation in each family, who must try to understand that their mother, sister, aunt or grandmother has not only been violently taken but continues to be inhumanly disrespected and disregarded after her death—one of the many blights in Canada's history and a present-day reality that Prime Minister Harper and others pretend does not exist.

On the hardest and heaviest days, I think not only of my own family's experience, but of the many Indigenous families who need support after experiencing such a loss, but do not have it. I think of families like Maisy Odjick's and Shannon Alexander's, who for years have been searching for their missing daughters who disappeared without a trace.

With the increasing visibility of MMIW in recent years, one of the building debates we see in the media and in parliament is about the need for an inquiry into MMIW. After asking other families of missing and murdered loved ones, I found, amidst a range of responses, a number of truths that we agree upon. Whether we call it an inquiry, a commission or an action plan, this process must first and foremost take its direction and leadership from the families of MMIW. Of course, dealing with this widespread issue will inevitably include a variety of segments of society—academics, politicians, community advocates, lawyers and police—but the inclusion and involvement of families must not be tokenistic, as it often has been.

An inquiry shouldn't focus just on confirming what we already know—that this is a widespread societal problem—but an inquiry should include community-based and Indigenous-led solutions. Unless a wide spectrum of families and communities are involved from the onset of such a plan, it will not succeed. It is

families and communities of MMIW who best understand the breadth, depth and root causes of this issue,
and what solutions could and should look like.

If there is an inquiry, it is also necessary to examine
how the police are dealing with the cases of MMIW and
to require that the RCMP and local police departments
share their files with families, especially when cases are
unsolved and idle like my sister's case. It is imperative
that we develop and implement policies that prevent
the inaction that makes the police complicit in allowing
the number of MMIW to grow. With so many cases
unsolved, it appears to those who murder and disappear
Indigenous women that there are no significant consequences. Also, justice is lacking for families when cases
are brought before the courts.

Another unknown in this polarizing debate is what
exactly an inquiry would entail. If its goal were to deter-
mine whether or not the police have been doing their
due diligence to solve the cases of MMIW, and to give
a comparative analysis of time spent on the cases of
MMIW versus time spent on those of non-Indigenous
women, then I might be inclined to agree that an inquiry
would be useful. But if millions of dollars are going to
be spent simply to verify whether the issue of MMIW
is a problem, then no. We do not need more research in
order to acknowledge that this is a serious problem we
need to address.

What we do need is to recognize that violence
against Indigenous women has systemic causes that are

colonial in nature. This is why books like this one are so important. Emmanuelle Walter brings to life the stories of two young girls to show the vibrant and multifaceted humanity that exists in our communities instead of the often dehumanizing, one-dimensional stories we read in the media about Indigenous women. *Stolen Sisters* documents how difficult the experiences are for families after a loved one is missing or murdered, by giving the reader an idea of how little support families often have when dealing with police inaction on cases. Her book also helps to dissect the root causes, which date back to colonial origins. The fact that wider Canadian society is not aware of these causes exacerbates the stereotypes of Indigenous communities and is part of why Indigenous women go missing or are murdered.

There are already close to sixty research papers on the issue of MMIW, and over seven hundred recommendations have already been put forward. Yet only a few of these recommendations have been implemented to date. Not only are these types of solutions needed, but we will need generations of healing for our communities to be healthy and whole again after this trauma. This violence against our women has lasted for hundreds of years— really since colonialism started on this continent.

Indigenous communities do not need to be studied to death. We need to be empowered to make the changes that we ourselves see fit for our Nations, communities and families. The federal government needs to recognize the impact that government policies have had and continue to have on Indigenous communities, in ways that leave Indigenous women in precarious and vulnerable positions in society. Until the government recognizes the root causes of violence against Indigenous women, their so-called action plan will never succeed.

The Tories' Action Plan, released on September 15, 2014, places the blame on Indigenous communities by insinuating that violence against our women happens solely within our communities. This is far from the truth. Violence is also inflicted upon our women by non-Indigenous men. This is a Canadian problem, not solely a First Nations problem.

We need to unpack the patriarchal, racist and colonial mentalities of Canadian society to ultimately address the reasons why Indigenous women's lives are not valued in Canadian society as much as the lives of white women. We need to hold those who perpetrate violence against women accountable. At least 1,200 Indigenous women have been murdered or have gone missing in the last thirty years alone. As Widia Larivière, co-founder of the Quebec branch of the Idle No More movement, has pointed out, if you look at this in terms of proportion of the population, this number of Indigenous women would represent around thirty thousand Canadian women. There is no denying that if thirty thousand white women were missing or had been murdered, there would be an uproar and the government's approach would be instantaneous and dramatic. A far cry from the current response.

A better approach would be to support spaces for healing from the legacy of trauma instead of continuing the victim-blaming narrative that we see from the Conservative government and the RCMP report, which released biased and misleading statistics in both 2014 and 2015. This attempt to blame the victim is in itself a form of systemic violence and does not place any responsibility on the RCMP for their inaction on these cases throughout the decades. These statistics are never linked to foundational root causes or driven to hold Canadian society accountable.

We continue to see principles of patriarchy embedded in the old colonial values that play out in Canadian society today. For example, the industrial system of resource extraction in Canada is predicated on systems of power and domination. This system is based on the raping and pillaging of Mother Earth as well as violence against women. The two are inextricably linked. With the expansion of extractive industries, not only do we see desecration of the land, we see an increase in violence against women. Rampant sexual violence against women and a variety of social ills result from the influx of transient workers in and around workers' camps. In capitalistic and ultra-conservative governments like Stephen Harper's—which have a pro–tar sands, mining, arctic drilling and fracking agenda—we see a disregard for the sacredness of this earth, just as we see a lack of care or concern for the hundreds of murdered and missing Indigenous women across the land.

Not only does the Tories' "action plan" not address the violence that we see in the unsafe industrialized zones, but it places the blame on Indigenous women and communities. On a trip to the Arctic in August 2014, when Harper was once again questioned about MMIW, he responded: "I think we should not view this as a sociological phenomenon. We should view it as a crime." This perspective completely ignores the relationship between colonization and the root causes of violence against women.

While we wait for politicians to debate the issues of MMIW and continue our push for change, we must also find ways to make all of our communities safer. It is essential that communities rise up and take back control of our Nations to ensure that our women are safe. Women are the life-givers of our Nations and the very fabric of who we are. I ask that we, Indigenous and non-Indigenous peoples, come together to demand the respect and dignity that Indigenous women deserve, and also that we help one another heal in these difficult times.

We have work to do regardless of what the government does: we need to rebuild, heal and restore what we have lost. Colonial violence is alive and well, but Indigenous peoples are strong and courageous, and will continue to push back against these daily realities. All of us are needed in this work to rebuild our communities, families and Nations.

The stories and the message in this book will help to push for this change. *Stolen Sisters* engages the audience and pulls them into the untold stories of MMIW and the families left behind. It will also help the Canadian public to understand more deeply the issues of MMIW and to feel the gross injustice that has been inflicted upon Indigenous women throughout Canadian history. Emmanuelle Walter weaves seamlessly between the stories of Maisy's and Shannon's disappearances, and intertwines both the historical and contemporary colonial root causes of murdered and missing Indigenous women and girls.

The day my sister passed away was the day Toronto became an unsafe place for me, filled with memories of pain and loss. When I let myself feel the horror and the pain from that day, I am reminded of all the memories that Bella and I had together growing up and all the future moments we will not share. Bella will not be there the day I finally bring a child into this world, and my children will never know her, or be able to look into her eyes, or call her aunty. I know this experience is not unlike that of the many hundreds of family members who live this grief-stricken reality.

Despite this, I will continue to do this work in honour of my sister and all the women who have lost their lives. I pray for justice and healing for the families of Maisy Odjick and Shannon Alexander and for all families across this land who have suffered the immense loss of their loved ones.

Melina Laboucan-Massimo

Introduction

In August 2014, as I was finishing this book for publication in Quebec and France, Tina died.

She was found by chance, on August 17, wrapped in a plastic bag and floating in the Red River. A beautiful, frail child of Winnipeg's streets, seen by police and taken into the care of child services a few short days before her disappearance, yet still falling through holes in the safety net, holes of ignorance, incompetence and racism. The death of Tina Fontaine—Ojibwe, fifteen years old, a runaway, a young girl lost, her father beaten to death in 2011, raised by a brave aunt—seemed particularly intolerable.

I had been working for over a year on the tragedy of missing and murdered Indigenous women. An immersion in the dark waters of injustice, horror, silence. I discovered the magnitude of the feminicide—a twofold phenomenon whereby countless women are murdered solely because of their gender, and government negligence further exacerbates the impact. Our social consensus–loving

Canada is without a shadow of a doubt the scene of what is a near-silent feminicide.

I never imagined that, this time, the country would respond. Yet Winnipeg's police chief pronounced his *mea culpa* with tears in his eyes, promising to improve procedures and reminding the public of the weight of the colonial past. Journalists did what they do when young white girls go missing: they listened to the family at length, investigated the circumstances surrounding the disappearance. The federal government agreed to hold a Round Table on the tragedy of these MMIW—Missing and Murdered Indigenous Women. At last, something was being done.

This book came out in its French edition on November 6, 2014. Two days later, two construction workers came across a young girl with long black hair lying unconscious on the banks of the Assiniboine River, in Winnipeg once again. Rinelle Harper, Cree, sixteen years old.

Brutally beaten and sexually assaulted, thrown into the water, Rinelle managed to pull herself out of the icy river only to be beaten again; she regained consciousness in hospital. Without the intervention of those chance passersby, she would have died. Hers was a return from the dead—had she caught a glimpse of the departed in the shadows? She made the decision to speak out in their name, publicly demanding on several occasions that an inquiry be held into the feminicide that refuses to speak its name. Media and the

Opposition relayed Rinelle's words. Through this long-haired warrior woman, tiny cracks began to show in the mantle of lead I denounced in the book. She would be seen a few months later during the Round Table on February 27, 2015, sitting shyly next to the Assembly of First Nations' national chief.

The awakening was, however, in no way chance's doing, but the product of the perseverance of Indigenous activists who, too often, are also the mothers, daughters, sisters, cousins and friends of murdered and missing women. I met with these women. Grief did not lay them low. In their sorrow they found the makings of their political battle. The media coverage of recent months is in large part due to their resilience and persistence. A long road lies ahead still. We cannot ignore the words spoken by Prime Minister Stephen Harper soon after Tina's death—"We should not view this as a sociological phenomenon. We should view it as a crime";[1] and, regarding the need for a national inquiry, "Um, it isn't really high on our radar, to be honest."[2] Despite repeated demands from the provinces and territories as well as from Indigenous and international organizations, the Harper government has isolated itself in its continued denial of the phenomenon. Shortly before and just after the Round Table, three new reports—one from the Organization of American States,[3] a second from the Legal Strategy Coalition on Violence Against Indigenous Women,[4] and a third . . . from the United Nations[5]—affirmed in quick succession the social and post-colonial nature of the feminicide and the need for large-scale reform to bring an end to the violence.

As I write these lines in the spring of 2015, reform is nowhere on the agenda.

Since the publication of this book in French, more names have been added to the list of victims. Brandy Mariah Vittrekwa, seventeen, murdered in Whitehorse on December 8, 2014; Angela Marie Poorman, twenty-nine, stabbed to death on December 15 in Winnipeg; Monica Lee Burns, twenty-eight, murdered in Prince Albert on January 17, 2015. And others still.

Of course, these women and girls remind me of two in particular, aged sixteen and seventeen, Maisy Odjick and Shannon Alexander. It is their story I tell in this book. The two young girls disappeared together from Maniwaki, Quebec, on September 6, 2008.

Maisy and Shannon were like sisters. Maisy lived on the Algonquin reserve of Kitigan Zibi, Shannon in a Maniwaki neighbourhood bordering the reserve. I see in their lovely faces an embodiment of this national tragedy. To tell their story is to tell the story of 1,181 Indigenous women murdered or gone missing in Canada between the years 1980 and 2012.[6] On many occasions, I was warned that any attempt to delve into the Indigenous world risked running into a brick wall. Nothing of the sort happened to me. Activists, families, Indigenous police, the reserve chief, men and women alike have been committed to keeping the girls' memory alive and giving voice to their own suffering, questions and anger.

Here, now, is the story of Maisy and Shannon, two joyful, rebellious and vulnerable girls.

Here, now, is the blind spot in a prosperous country, Canada.

I

PITOBIG STREET, KITIGAN ZIBI
January 11, 2014

A house and its unfinished white siding, topped by a cable dish, surrounded by nothing but fog, snow, ghostly birch trees and, across the road, a lake.

I passed right by, driving near blind, unable to read a single street number. On Quebec's Kitigan Zibi Anishinabeg reserve, 18,000 hectares of land 140 kilometres north of Ottawa, the homes of its 1,500 residents are, for the most part, dotted along small roads running through the forest; the "streets" go on forever. I pulled a U-turn, taking up the icy width of Pitobig Street, then retraced my route, waving back at other drivers who, in the fog, thought they were crossing paths with someone from the community—who else would be driving out here?

Then, there it was to the left, at the top of a slippery slope. I left the car down below.

The street where Lisa Odjick, Maisy's grandmother, lives.

It was in September 2013 in Maniwaki, during the annual walk in memory of Maisy and Shannon, the two friends who had disappeared together five years earlier, that I first came upon Lisa Odjick, "Little Grandma," sitting on a bench in the warm fall air. A small, gentle grandmother with short grey hair, burdened by time's passing and the forever ache that began with the disappearance of her granddaughter Maisy.

Now, four months later, I find Lisa busy cooking—her former trade—making meatloaf. We speak in French.

"When I was five, we moved to the edge of the reserve; across the way my neighbours were white, Québécois. So I learned French. Back then, we didn't have electricity. I'd go to their place to watch TV!" She laughs.

Everything is simple here, a bit rickety, makeshift, but Lisa makes do. She can't count all the houses and flats she's lived in on the reserve; life goes by too fast. Lisa tells me about her mother, who died of a hemorrhage when she was only six months old ("We lived deep in the woods, she couldn't be saved"); about her unsettled and precarious life, from an adoptive mother to residential school to foster families; Abitibi, Quebec City, the reserve; a year in the States, where her only daughter, Laurie, Maisy's mother, was born; and back to the reserve in the early '70s.

It is here, in Lisa's home, between the lake and the forest, that Maisy spent many months; it was here that she lived before vanishing into thin air. The walls in the small living room are covered with pictures. Big sister Maisy, almond eyes, delicate features, radiant smile, her arms around her three brothers and sister. Papoose Maisy, wearing a traditional red dress and matching headscarf. Maisy in her graduation gown and its native designs, posing with her diploma. Teen Maisy, with blonde highlights.

"Maisy lived with her boyfriend for a while, but it wasn't working out; she called Earl, my husband, and said, 'Come get me.' She was almost sixteen. She moved in with us, she wasn't happy with her mother. She'd dropped out of school."

"What was it like living with Maisy?"

"I loved it. I loved her company. She turned part of the basement into her bedroom with sheets she hung from the ceiling for walls. We had fun together, we talked, we played cards, Crazy Eights . . . We'd sit in those armchairs" (she points, one beige, one pomegranate), "and watch our favourite shows: *Next Top Model*, singing contests, we didn't want to miss any . . . She did collages with the computer, she drew . . . She came up with new hairdos and took pictures, selfies . . ." (Lisa laughs, pretends to pose for a camera, then brings out a few pictures to show me). "Look at this one here" (a magnificent Maisy with blue dreadlocks). "This is my favourite picture. She'd help me some. She was learning to cook—little things, spaghetti sauce, macaroni, easy stuff. I think about her all the time . . . It's so hard. She was like my daughter . . ."

"Like another Laurie, then."

"We loved that girl the minute she came into the world. Maisy, our first grandchild. During the birth, the first time we saw her, her tiny head . . . My husband was so moved he couldn't speak."

*
*   *
*

Maisy's little brother Damon, two years her junior, comes up from the basement. It's his turn to live here after leaving home, his turn to drive his mother crazy by refusing to go to school; his turn to take comfort in Little Grandma's gentle ways and appetizing meals. It's also his turn to live in the basement that he quietly refuses to let me see; "It's too messy." Bit by bit, Damon describes his big sister in a few carefully chosen words: "special, funny, talked a lot, never alone." He adds that Maisy lived for a while in Ontario too, with their father, Rick Jacko, Laurie's first husband.

Suddenly, Damon disappears downstairs, then returns with a big black plastic box. Lisa comes closer, puts on her glasses. With barely a word, they bring out objects that used to belong to Maisy and lay them on the table one by one.

Lisa Odjick's house, where Maisy lived for a time.

A clarinet in a dust-covered case.

A small Native doll in blue with a red-beaded band around her forehead.

A 2005 certificate for Ojibwe, the Algonquin language, from the Southampton school in Ontario, where the family lived for three years.

Family picture albums made by Maisy.

A blue cardboard box that Lisa said "she took everywhere with her," filled with dozens of pictures, including a black and white shot of Maisy, her head resting on her boyfriend's shoulder.

A science notebook filled with her round handwriting and, inside, a typed assignment marked 8 out of 10, with the comment "Good."

Class notes from September 2007, just a few weeks before she decided to drop out.

A white picture frame in the shape of a dog, with a baby picture.

A picture frame shaped like a wolf, with a picture of her little sister wearing a pink dress.

"Sometimes Maisy looked sad," Lisa says. "Sometimes she said she didn't deserve to be loved. I always told her she had every right to be loved. And that our hearts would be broken if anything ever happened to her."

She stops, unable to continue.

"I'd tell Maisy not to waste her life, and then she decided to go back to school."

From a drawer, she pulls out one of the treasured handwritten notes that Maisy used to leave on the table. *Gone again!* and in her round letters, *Call you later. Love, Maisy.*

KOKO STREET, MANIWAKI
August 2008

"I was leaving to go back to Ottawa," Pam told me. "A few weeks before they disappeared, I'd gone to see my son Bryan and my granddaughter Shannon in their apartment on Koko Street in Maniwaki.

"Shannon walked out ahead of me, was sitting on top of the dog house at Bryan's house. Her legs were crossed. She had a cute short haircut, really short, and she was so pretty. That was the last time I saw her.

"She said, 'Grandma, are you going to leave?'

"I said 'Yes.'

"'And are you going back to Ottawa?'

"I said 'Yes.'

"'Can I come back to Ottawa with you?'

"I said 'No, I'm not going to be in Ottawa for long. I'm leaving for my job.' She couldn't come."

At the time, Pam worked as a senior policy analyst for the Canadian army and was in charge of hiring

Indigenous employees. She looked after monitoring and assessing her young recruits. "I was responsible for the Aboriginal portfolio so if anything happened, when there was an issue, I had to go and see what it was. Look into it, investigate it. See what could be done to mediate or whatever. I worked for the army for fifteen years. It took up a lot of my time."

Beyond the park, the apartment where Shannon lived with her father on Koko Street in Maniwaki, and where the girls were seen for the very last time.

* * * *

Pam. Pamela. Elegant, grey curls, doing her accounting in her Kitigan Zibi home on Highway 105. The other grandmother, Shannon Alexander's grandmother. Pam, who was always travelling back and forth between the reserve and her Ottawa apartment, 140 km to the south; Pam who, fortunately for me, was at home one January afternoon, on one of those icy days when just setting foot outside means running the risk of breaking a leg; Pam, who told me brusquely from behind the screen door to shoo the cat from the doorstep if I expected her to open the door; she was allergic, there was no way that cat was getting inside.

I reached for the big cat and it tore down the steps.

She softened when she understood why I had come.

"My name is Pam Mitchell Sickles."

"Sickles? S-i-c-k-l-e-s?"

"Yeah. I'm seventy." She continued: "My mother was from Kitigan Zibi. My dad from Akwesasne, a reserve on the border. My father was Mohawk, my mother Algonquin. I was born in Ottawa, where they met. They were in a tuberculosis sanatorium together."

Then we got to the heart of the matter.

"You know, Shannon was a very attractive girl. Seventeen years old. Her pictures look . . . but she was a beautiful girl. Very tall, very slender. And she moved very . . ."

Yes, I knew.

The missing-person posters described Maisy as 6 foot tall, Shannon as 5 foot 9; 125 lbs for M., 145 lbs for S. They show Maisy's radiant face, Shannon's moodier one. Two tall, graceful, resourceful young women who spent most of their time together despite differing backgrounds. Maisy lived with her family—her brothers and her sister;

her mother, Laurie, a radio host for the reserve's station; and her stepfather, Mark, who worked at the general store. Shannon was born in Ottawa to a drug-addicted mother, Caroline, and to Bryan, Pam's son, about whom I knew little at the time, other than that he was in a bad way, suffering from alcoholism. One of the missing posters shows a stunning Shannon, her gaze intense, wearing a beret from the army cadets, a scout-like organization she'd belonged to since the age of twelve.

"When Shannon was a baby," Pam continued, "Caroline left. Caroline and Bryan wanted me to take Shannon and have her stay with me. They asked me several times while she was growing up. But I worked for the Canadian forces. I live alone, my husband died and I had to work, and I travelled a lot with my job. My hours were different. I would have had to quit my job. I don't feel guilty about that, you know. When my daughter, Bryan's sister, finally asked to keep her for the school year, Bryan wouldn't . . . He raised Shannon alone, he was crazy about her. There was no more talk of her living anywhere else."

*
* *
*

Pam interrupts her story from time to time to mention the cat, a tabby. "Look at that cat looking at us through the window . . . She wants to come in, but as soon as she's inside, my allergies act up. If it gets to minus 18 I'll bring her in, but . . . It's my brother's cat . . . He didn't believe me that I was allergic, but once he saw me, he said 'Wow!' So the cat stays outside."

It seemed that, more than grief, Pam was battling her guilt and her own tough edge. But later, listening to the interview on my recorder, I would hear her stifled sobs, her trembling voice. I would hear her pronounce the following sentence matter-of-factly, out of the blue: "When you love someone, you tell them you love them, you tell them you care about them. You never know when you might lose them."

"Whenever I came to stay in Kitigan Zibi, Shannon would come over, sleep over, she'd be sitting here and tell me how mad she was at her father, who loved her, who was doing his best, but who drank, and made her clean up her room, do her own laundry—that's how I raised him and his brothers and sister. Then it'd be time to go to bed and Shannon'd go over, call her father and say, 'I love you, Dada, good night,' as curt as could be." (Pam mimicked an exasperated teen, then burst out laughing.) "Watching Shannon go up the stairs, she'd just be shaking she was so mad at her father."

I told Pam I hadn't dared approach Bryan when I saw him at the commemorative event in Maniwaki, wearing a light grey sweater, beige pants and white running shoes, beer can in hand, his head shaved, the ravaged features of someone whose life is no life. He barely managed to make his way up to the mic. I don't remember what he said. He'd been speaking for less than a minute when a huge sob cut his words short. He pushed his way through the crowd to escape.

"I'll call," Pam said after a moment's thought. "Yeah, I'll call him. He should be home, it's raining."

On the first try, she dialled the wrong number. Then, "Hi, Bryan? This is your mother speaking. Okay. Anyhow . . ." (a little laugh), "there's a journalist here. She'd like to speak to you. She wants to write a book." (She stresses the word *book*). "About Shannon's disappearance. And I think it's the best way to get the story out about Shannon." (If only I could be so sure.) "I don't know the story, and you're the only one that could tell her."

Just as Bryan replied, a screech of violins sounded on the radio.

"But she's putting it into a book."

All of a sudden, she hung up. "He says, 'If she wants to talk to me she can come and talk to me, but I'm tired of telling people the story.' He's angry. As usual."

3
Nagishkodadiwin Park, Maniwaki
September 6, 2013

We walked for five kilometres, from Kitigan Zibi to the centre of Maniwaki. Laurie, Maisy's mother, teased me about the wedge sandals I was wearing when everyone else had running shoes on. Could there have been one hundred, two hundred of us?—families, the reserve chief, part of the Algonquin community, the federal NDP member, the provincial Liberal member; Amnesty International staff from Ottawa; activists from Families of Sisters in Spirit, the association of families of missing and murdered Indigenous women; a representative from Enfant-Retour Québec, the Quebec branch of the Missing Children Society; a few local journalists. We walked along Highway 105 just as on every other year on the same date in memory of Maisy and Shannon, five years after their disappearance.

No shouting, no slogans, no anger; a quiet walk through a town, deserted right now, as the dinner hour approached. Participants hugged and smiled at one another, their children cheerfully weaving between the sidewalk and the front yards; reserve residents honked in solidarity as they drove home—all sound and movement made to mask despair. Mark, Maisy's stepfather, wore the poster showing Shannon around his neck; Maisy's little sister wore the poster for her big sister; Bryan, Shannon's father, dazed, pale, silent, wore his fury. A van bearing the banner "Missing" and a likeness of the two girls crawled along beside them.

It was almost 6:30 in Nagishkodadiwin Park, an Algonquin community development in the centre of Maniwaki. The evening's vigil began by the glow of candles set up around the bandstand. At the mic, Annie, Laurie's aunt by marriage, elderly and stately, prayed in Algonquin, then spoke of the changes she'd seen in the small town since the girls' disappearance: she felt that it had become dangerous and cold. Laurie stood off to the side, facing her aunt. She drew closer, as though to better hear the speakers' words, thank them for their presence and experience this moment of solidarity and solitude in all its intensity.

Suddenly, she turned her head. A woman and a child of about ten were crossing the street bearing hand drums. Time stood still. Our silent gathering watched Laurie walk toward them and hug them close. Then the woman and child stepped onto the bandstand, pulled out traditional whistles and whistled to the four cardinal directions, nodding over and over. I assumed because of the delicate features and long braids that the child was a girl, but it was in fact a boy, an amazing young boy named Theland, who began chanting in his language with the same inflections I had heard at other ceremonies, with only the low notes posing a problem for him, as they would have for any other youngster. English came next and Laurie, stoic till then, dissolved into tears and sought refuge in her son's arms.

The bandstand at Nagishkodadiwin Park, Maniwaki.

When the sun went down the moon
*   and stars were out*
It was a beautiful night
I saw a shooting star

I started thinking of you
Until I see you again, you're always in my heart.

It was my first time in Maniwaki, a small town of four thousand in western Quebec, not far from the Ontario border. To get there, I followed Highway 15 north from Montreal, then Highway 117, the road through the Upper Laurentians. Rounded green mountains linked together like a giant spinal column, fir trees, marshes, food trucks, dilapidated motels, the Manoir de Picardie restaurant, more fir trees, lakes, cottages, windshield doctors (*Esthétique voitures et bateaux, docteur du pare-brise*), rundown mobile homes, giant closed indoor flea markets, more fir trees, impassive lakes, fishing outfitters (*Tout pour la pêche, le paradis du pêcheur*), trailer sales, the *Bar-spectacle Saint-François*, featuring nude dancers, more fir trees and lakes. Swimming pools were empty, schoolgrounds full; chairlifts swayed in the breeze, forlorn; the touristless Laurentians awaited both skiers and snow.

Grand Remous is already part of the Outaouais. Turn left onto Highway 105 South. A barely perceptible change in scenery: slightly more farmland, gentler, less mountainous. Here is Maniwaki and its Indigenous neighbour, Kitigan Zibi Anishinabeg, the Algonquin reserve—KZA to locals. Two small towns pressed up against each other, one white, inhabited by 4,000 Francophones, the other Indigenous, inhabited by 1,600 Anglophones.

I was to meet the co-founder of Families of Sisters in Spirit, a support group for the families of the disappeared, in front of the neighbourhood Home Hardware. Bridget Tolley was a resident of Kitigan Zibi and a born organizer who was always on the go; she had organized the commemoration with Laurie.

Highway 117 crosses the Upper Laurentians and runs north of Kitigan Zibi.

The hardware store was closed for good.

Bridget parked next to me. She was just back from Ottawa, where she'd tried to find Caroline, Shannon's mother, to bring her to the walk; she had searched for her in her neighbourhood with no luck. "That's okay," said Bridget, as though to say, "I don't hold it against her, not being here," knowing what she did of Caroline's drug addiction and how lost she was. Bridget and I leaned against our cars in the cool early-September breeze as we spoke. Then, like a thunderbolt come from the sky, a blue T-shirt emerged striding purposefully. "This is Laurie," Bridget said. "Laurie Odjick."

Laurie was the first to say yes. Yes to telling me the story of the disappearance of her daughter Maisy and of her daughter's best friend, Shannon. Yes to a return to that cataclysmic time, to her anger at the police and the media, to her feelings of overwhelming solitude, to her fight for the families, to her shattered life. Yes to representing, whatever her misgivings, the mothers of Canada's missing Indigenous daughters. Yes, no conditions attached, no special demands, just yes.

"You know something?" Laurie said. "One day, I picked up a guy from the reserve looking for a ride, a guy they suspected after Maisy and Shannon went missing."

We were sitting under a huge wooden shelter on the shores of Lake Pocknock the day after the walk. Out of the drizzle. It was "Family Day," fair day on the reserve with a fishing contest on the lake, bingo, bum-scooting races; we ate steak, potatoes and salad. Beside Laurie sat Mark, her second husband, the father of her two youngest children, and a source of unfailing support—one of those men of few words who do so much more—watching the children run this way and that.

"The guy was walking towards Maniwaki and it is our community so . . . He stopped at a crosswalk and I'm like . . ."

"You wondered what you would do?"

"It was more like, what do I have the courage to do?"

For a few months, it was a policeman from Mont-Laurier, a town 168 kilometres to the northeast, who was in charge of the Maisy/Shannon case. Long enough to bungle things badly: Laurie told me he whispered the names of two suspects to her—two young Indigenous men from the community.

"Young men you knew?"

"Yes, of course."

"Ones you saw regularly?"

"Yes. I had to live with it. The fact he told me the names . . . there's a lot of anger there. What if I got mad . . . and did whatever? I would have been in jail . . ."

At that time, it had been two or three years—Laurie wasn't exactly sure how long—since the two young men had been questioned. Nothing came of it.

She stopped her car. "I think I wanted to see how he reacted when he recognized me. At that moment when I picked him up on the side of the road, it was not my truck. And when he got in . . ."

Laurie took a deep breath, as though suffocating, "I said, 'Hi, how are you, blah, blah, blah.' He said, 'I'm doing fine, etc.' I thought, 'What if it was him?' I was tempted to, you know . . . to talk about it . . . He kind of put me at ease. Somebody who would have done something to my daughter wouldn't be so at ease. Unless he was that evil."

"'Cause he knew that you knew he'd been questioned by police?"

"He knew that I knew."

"Are the two of them bad kids, delinquents?"

"I won't say anything about them. Did I think they were involved? When you've lost a child, it's hard to think straight. But deep down, I don't think it was them."

As I drove through the rain that day, suffering and sorrow seemed to hover above the car like ghosts; it came to me that Laurie had lost Maisy not just once, but three times. Once when she left home to live with her boyfriend at the age of fifteen. Again, when she chose to live with her grandmother. And finally, when she disappeared at the age of sixteen going on seventeen.

"Could it all have turned out differently?" Laurie wondered. "Like, if we hadn't moved back from Saugeen?"

* *
*

Saugeen is Mark's community, on the shores of Lake Huron in Ontario, 800 km from Maniwaki. The family—Laurie, Mark and the four children—lived there for three years after Mark found a job as a social worker. There is no school on the reserve, so the children did their schooling in Southampton, the neighbouring town, where Maisy made good friends. "She was very close to the white girls," Laurie pointed out, as though to say that wasn't necessarily a given; she excelled in sports and, on the cusp of adolescence, was coming into her own, Maisy-style, stubborn, rebellious, "*tête dure*," Laurie said in French, with a laugh.

Laurie went for training in geriatric care, then started up a small accounting business. But for Mark, whose job meant placing underprivileged or abused children from the reserve in foster homes, life became impossible. "He'd be the one to go into homes to remove the children. He had a hard time doing that in his own community. One day, he said he just couldn't do it anymore."

Mark found himself at the heart of a tragedy deeply rooted in the history of the First Nations; over the course of more than a hundred years, 150,000 Indigenous children in Canada were removed from their families by law enforcement officers and placed in residential schools designed with the express purpose of "taking the Indian out of the child," places where hunger and abuse were commonplace. Another practice followed on its heels: that of deliberately placing children in white families at great distances from their communities; this was the "Sixties Scoop," which affected twenty thousand children, a period that lasted from the 1960s to the 1980s. Today 30 to 40 percent of all children placed in care are Indigenous, although they account for only 5 percent of all Canadian children.[1] More often than not, they end up living outside their culture and their community. Too often, the reason for their placement is not abuse but poverty.

So Mark decided to quit his job.

"Me, I missed my parents," Laurie added. "So in 2006, we came back to Kitigan Zibi. Maisy never really accepted the move, and that's when our big fight started. A big, big fight."

How to bring up a teen in an Indigenous community, even among the least devastated, where both past (cultural annihilation, forced migration, the removal of children, destroyed families) and present trauma (lack of employment, of a future, of meaning) together contribute to drop-out rates, mental health issues, violence and self-harm? How to bring up a teen who sees alcoholism, despair and defeat on a daily basis? The adults I met on the reserve made no effort to hide the fact that many of their young people go through an alcohol/drug/drop-out phase.

So Laurie, now an addictions counsellor in Kitigan Zibi, found herself in the same situation as Mark had been in Saugeen: trying to cure the hurts and ills of her community. "It's really tough," she confided one day.

What to do? Leave? In Canada, half of all Indigenous people live off reserve, but not without a struggle. The reserve is also the only place where they can safeguard what remains of social, family and psychological ties, and pass down traditions to their children. At the worst times of her life, during that first year after her daughter's disappearance, when the ground was continually threatening to swallow her whole, Laurie chose to stay in her community. Maybe because the community of

Kitigan Zibi Anishinabeg has been able to hold its own. It is too far from large urban centres and the American border to be a regular hideout for drug traffickers and smugglers, yet close enough to Ottawa, the capital, to avoid the appalling poverty-stricken isolation of reserves farther to the north. KZA has had competent chiefs; the reserve has its own police force, daycare, radio station, schools, scholarships and women's shelter. Its maple syrup is exported as far afield as New Zealand. It has logging, a cultural centre and a political elite that includes a researcher with the University of Ottawa, a women's activist, a young up-and-coming Indigenous politician, and others still. And Chief Whiteduck, one of Eastern Canada's Indigenous leaders, has banked on education and won recognition for Kitigan Zibi's high school diploma by Ontario and Quebec colleges.

So Laurie decided to believe. To start working for community radio, then in health services. To defend the right to educate her children in the community. And to bring up teen Maisy. Maisy the seamstress, who made her pow wow regalia all on her own—Laurie sent me a picture of the outfit Maisy made for herself at the age of twelve, pink and purple fabric adorned with flower and butterfly designs—Maisy who loved to read, play dress-up with her brothers and sister, and decorate the house for each birthday. Maisy, too, who drank, smoked marijuana, had moody spells, stole money from her mother and wanted to ditch everything, starting with school.

"She told me she was taking a year off," Laurie said with a hint of a smile (Laurie always has that same ironic glint in her eye). "At fifteen . . ."

We were talking over breakfast at the Rialdo café in Maniwaki. "The problems started with Maisy because she asked if her boyfriend could sleep over at home. And I said no. 'Cause she was too young. Then another day a few weeks later she tried again, in front of him. I said no. 'If he has to leave, I'm leaving, too,' Maisy said. I said, 'Okay, see you later.' I tried to act tough. My daughter packed her bags and I cried, but not in front of her."

The reserve's social services came to the house at Laurie's request only to tell her, "Yes, teens can leave home at the age of fifteen, but welfare won't pay anything." Maisy moved in with Derek's family, Algonquin as well, and then with Derek himself, who, being older, lived on his own. Where? "In town somewhere," Laurie said, unwilling to dwell on the subject. In town meant Maniwaki. On the main street, in fact, behind the pizzeria, close to the hospital.

"I helped her a little bit 'cause I wanted to stay in her life. We talked and talked. Then, once she had a good taste of reality and some independence . . . she moved in with my mom. Little Grandma gave more freedom than me, which was okay. I was happy she was under my mother's roof."

*
* *
*

Night has fallen on Nagishkodadiwin Park. At the mic, Bridget has sent out a plea for Maisy and Shannon's return home. The two politicians have called for a national inquiry into missing and murdered Indigenous women, an oft-made request to which the Harper government continues to turn a deaf ear. I hop onto one of the buses shuttling the sad, silent walkers back to the Home Hardware parking lot. Bryan has disappeared.

4
HIGHWAY 105
April 12, 2014

One Saturday at noon, with snow melting and deer venturing out of the woods by the dozen, a sober, smiling Bryan, infected perhaps by the warm advent of spring, welcomed me into his small white house set on concrete blocks along Highway 105. At the time of his daughter Shannon's disappearance, Bryan lived in town, in Maniwaki. Since then, however, he has moved onto the reserve, where he feels more at home. Shannon was present in a way, featured in a missing person poster that Bryan had hung to the right of the front door. I had waited months before summoning up the courage to approach him. I was leery of his alcoholism, his rage, and afraid I would reopen old wounds with my questions.

My fears were unfounded. Bryan—a tall, thin man with a moustache, gaunt cheeks and a boxer's nose—was still in pain, the wound still fresh. I would change nothing there. "If you come with Maria," he had told me, "that'll be fine." Maria Jacko is Maisy's aunt; since the girls disappeared, she and Bryan have become friends.

The house where Shannon's father, Bryan, lives on the reserve.

She accompanied me. All three of us sat down at the kitchen table. Until that point, it had looked like Shannon would end up being the young woman in the shadows, a secondary character, the girl whose portrait would not be fully fleshed out, but then she came to life with Bryan's words.

"Shannon went out with a boy for six or seven years, Matt, a good kid . . ."

"Six or seven years? You mean she was eleven when they started dating?"

"Uh-huh! They'd go out, then they'd break up, then they'd get back together again." Bryan smiled fondly. "His family had a farm and horses . . . The kid was allergic to horses, but Shannon loved to ride. She loved adventure! I could never stop her. I didn't want to stop her. Shannon always expected me to punish her when she did something wrong. If she broke something, I'd say, 'It's no big deal.' Then she'd scold me, 'Why don't you punish me? Other parents punish their kids!' I'd say, 'No, I'm not gonna punish you. If I do, you'll just go to your room and sneak out the window.' That made her mad. But my father beat the shit out of me when I was a kid, and I didn't want to do that to her."

"She wanted to go into nursing, is that right?"

Bryan got to his feet and poured himself a cup of coffee. "No, that's what I wanted!"

Maria and I laughed.

"She didn't know what to do . . . At cadets, they wanted her to be an officer. She was a real good marksman, I taught her how. But she wasn't interested. She knew it would mean a lot of responsibility. She quit cadets."

Shannon went to the Anglophone school in Maniwaki. "A very beautiful but very headstrong girl. Her father did what he could. Child services' social workers kept tabs on her," I had been told over the phone. At the age of sixteen, Shannon got into an argument with the principal over a bad mark in French that jeopardized her graduation. Bryan had this to say about the incident. "I told her, 'Shannon, you know what, I see potential in you. You go and see that principal and tell her you're quitting that fucking school. No one speaks French in my house, so they can just lay off you about French.' And she did. She got mad at the principal." (He laughed.) "Then I put her in Adult Ed and she graduated from French, all her French was done!"

Bryan told the media how Shannon, fifteen at the time, took the bus to Ottawa one day, followed directions from her friends and relatives who lived in Vanier, the capital's tough inner city, and found her mother, Caroline, in a crackhouse. "That really hit her hard. She flipped out and was never the same. She was quieter,"[1] he said. Caroline, an Inuit woman from Iqaluit, was an alcoholic and a drug addict and the mother of five other children, none of whom she lived with. When Bryan filled out a form for the Missing Children Society of Canada, an organization that offers support to the families of missing children, in regard to Caroline he wrote, "Address unknown—she lives in a shelter in Ottawa." I wanted to meet Caroline; Maria passed along my message, but Caroline declined.

It was Bryan who witnessed the growing friendship between Shannon and Maisy. "Maisy was at our place a lot," he explained. "From her grandmother's house, you just take the railway tracks and you're here in no time." They'd known each other for a while even though they didn't go to the same school. According to Bryan, their friendship grew from one specific incident.

"One day, a girl picked on Maisy in front of Shannon, called her a lesbian. Shannon stepped in to be her friend and protect her. She always stood up for gays. If kids started bugging Maisy, you can bet Shannon was all over them," he told Maria with a smile.

Maisy didn't hide her bisexuality. Besides Bryan, two other people—a friend and a family member—mentioned it to me. After she broke up with her boyfriend Derek, she reconnected with a young blond girl from her old Ontario school; she was in love. She'd visit her occasionally. So the term "free-spirited," used often by her parents and friends to describe Maisy, also referred to the way she lived her sexuality.

Shannon, also described as "free-spirited" (even on the form filled out for the Missing Children Society of Canada), was the one who defended other people's right to freely live their sexuality.

Bryan, from his front-row seat on the incandescent adolescent friendship, spoke as though it had all taken place just yesterday—with an ever-present half-smile, a tenderness that refused to be erased.

5
ON THE HILL
October 4, 2013

We were so alone on the streets of Ottawa and the steps of Parliament, just our little group surrounded by nothing but silence and wind; in the capital, at the feet of power, we demonstrated in a void of indifference. I look at my pictures and videos and see the wide open streets, the sparse audience, two police officers on their bikes our only escort; but the songs, the dances, the speeches and the tears, the consolation of being together, filled that void.

This is the way it is every October 4: a march on Parliament, punctuated by song and dance; then, at the top of the steps, the words of those bearing witness before a small but fervent audience. On that particular October 4, tired of repeating her story again and again, Laurie spoke only briefly of her daughter. Yet she hugged several women who broke down at the mic telling stories of bodies, arms and feet bound, found in the waters of the St. Lawrence River, young women burned, others murdered then thrown to the side of the road or battered to death by their spouses; the stories of mothers who had disappeared off the face of the earth.

Gathered together were the families of missing and murdered Indigenous women. In fact, there were two gatherings that day. At noon, an official event was organized by the Native Women's Association of Canada (NWAC) and attended by Liberal and NDP MPs and representatives from the Assembly of First Nations. The evening was devoted to a community event under the umbrella of the Families of Sisters in Spirit. An ideological rift existed between the two associations: the latter accused the former of kowtowing to the federal government. Families found they had to speak twice in the space of a few short hours, telling their stories over and over again.

Sisters in Spirit/*Sœurs par l'esprit*: missing and murdered women. "These are the women who left us under such tragic circumstances and by whose side we walk," explained Michèle Audette, NWAC president at the time. The same title was given to her association's database, which includes the names of over six hundred missing and murdered Indigenous women. The tragedy has its own hashtag, #MMIW, its own parliamentary reports, support groups and community workshops; its social media, activists, feminists, dissidents, commemorative plaques; and its sadly emblematic towns and sites, Canada's black holes (poor violent districts, deserted highways), marches and gatherings throughout the country. *A mari usque ad mare.*

Since 2006, Sisters in Spirit gatherings have taken place every year on October 4;[1] memory walks are held on February 14, the day in 1991 that Vancouver's Indigenous women began honouring all their missing and murdered sisters. A world of struggle and tears as densely populated, once one comes upon it, as it is invisible to the majority of Canadians.[2]

Yet the country is not unaware of the tragedy. Tina Fontaine's murder in August 2014 and the attack on Rinelle Harper in November lifted the veil on the high level of violence confronting young Indigenous girls in Winnipeg. It is embodied by Vancouver's Downtown Eastside (DTES), Canada's poorest neighbourhood—and not just the poorest. Every day in the 1990s, it saw at least one death by overdose; today, its rates of AIDS and hepatitis C are among the highest in the Western world;[3] here poverty, disease and violence are concentrated to an extraordinary degree. Among the many sex workers living in the DTES, most of whom are drug addicts, the majority are Indigenous women. It was here that serial killer Robert Pickton found his future victims; here too that the sheer number of murdered and missing sex workers, especially Indigenous women, eventually led to a targeted police investigation followed by a commission of inquiry into that investigation.[4]

Three of B.C.'s northern highways—Highway 16, dubbed the Highway of Tears, but also highways 5 and

97—embody the phenomenon as well. Between 1969 and 2006, forty-six women, most of them Indigenous, disappeared or were murdered here. For want of adequate and regular public transportation in the isolated mountainous regions, many of them had been hitchhiking. A month after the commission of inquiry into the murders of Indigenous women recommended increased funding for public transportation in the region, Greyhound Canada announced its plans to reduce the frequency of its buses by 40 percent. In her thesis on missing and murdered women and the Canadian justice system, researcher Maryanne Pearce underlines the frightening connection between the two; the dearth of public transportation makes it impossible for young Indigenous people in the region (over 15 percent of B.C.'s northern residents are Indigenous) to find work: their low incomes keep them from owning a car; without a car, they have to hitchhike and put themselves in harm's way. Late in the game, in 2009, the RCMP took stock of the situation and struck a special task force to investigate murders and disappearances along the Highway of Tears and other highways. Eighteen cases were chosen for closer scrutiny. After hundreds of DNA samples and more than two thousand interrogations, the E-PANA group was able to shed light on the cases of three young women.

So it is for Vancouver, regularly touted as one of the world's best cities to live in, and in the progressive and ecologically minded province of British Columbia, that a ghetto to the south and a highway fraught with danger to the north paint another picture.

And so it is that, in the Canada of milk and honey dreamed of by immigrant hopefuls the world over—where social consensus is an integral part of the national identity and the crime rate is among the lowest in the world—there lies a hidden face, the #MMIW tragedy.

On October 4, 2013, at the top of the steps to Parliament Hill, the time had come for that face to show itself as Thomas Mulcair, leader of the New Democratic Party and the Official Opposition, stated: "The number of women living in the Ottawa region is equal to the total number of Aboriginal women in Canada. If, in a city the size of Ottawa, 600 women were murdered or missing, do you really think there would have to be protests to get a national inquiry?"

He could have added that Indigenous women are seven times more likely to be murdered than non-Indigenous women.[5] Or cited the tally kept by the NWAC: 668 missing or murdered Indigenous women between 1980 and 2013, half of whom were under the age of thirty-one.[6] Or the 912 cases listed by Maryanne Pearce,[7] representing approximately one quarter of all missing or murdered women, while Indigenous women represent only 4.3 percent of all women in Canada.[8] In its 2009 report *No More Stolen Sisters,* Amnesty International rails: "Given the relatively small Indigenous population[9] and the overall low rate of violent crime in Canada, these numbers are truly appalling."

Several months after our gathering, in May of 2014,

the RCMP finally published its own numbers after surveying 300 police services across the country: 1,181 Indigenous women were either murdered or went missing between 1980 and 2012. As we have already seen, these women represented 23 percent of all female homicide victims in 2012.[10] Of the 1,181 women, 1,017 were killed and 164 are missing. The report—compiled within the ranks of the very police force that, up until then, had refused to believe the much lower numbers advanced by the NWAC—confirmed activists' worst fears.

But the best way to understand the extent of the phenomenon was to listen to Connie Greyeyes on that October day. Connie stood at the top of those same steps, emotional and despairing. She had not come from northern B.C. to tell her own story, that of a child torn from her parents, a young girl beaten and raped on more than one occasion, but the stories of eleven of her missing or murdered friends, neighbours, aunts, cousins. Eleven. Her tale boggles the mind. Few of us can say we know personally eleven murdered or missing people.[11] To be Connie is to live in a time of war and see your next of kin, your loved ones, your acquaintances disappear and die; to live with a knot of fear in your belly.

*
*   *
*

And so they go missing; and so they die. Indigenous women and girls are tightrope walkers working without a net. Domestic violence, community violence, street violence, sexual violence, racial violence—all threaten to unbalance them and topple them off.

They die at the hands of their spouses (Inusiq Aka-vak, 2000, Nunavut), neighbours or acquaintances (Crystal Bearisto, 2002, Prince Edward Island), and their cousins (Hilary Bonnelle, 2009, New Brunswick), but also at the hands of serial killers (Brenda Wolfe, 1999, B.C.). They die on highways, hitchhiking (Ramona Wilson, 1994, B.C.) or cycling (Monica Jack, 1978, B.C.); they die because they walk alone on the street and dare to be Indigenous (Helen Betty Osborne, 1971, Manitoba). Their bodies are found in their homes (Joanne Ghostkeeper, 1997, Alberta), in the mountains (Lynn Jackson, 2004, Alberta), in abandoned graveyards (Charlene Orshalak, 1988, Manitoba), in dumps (Courtney Johnstone, 2014, Alberta), in hockey bags (Loretta Saunders, 2014, New Brunswick), in frozen canals (Sandra Kaye Johnson, 1992, Ontario), under bridges (Tiffany Morrison, 2006, Quebec), in garbage bags (Carolyn Sinclair, 2012, Manitoba), on riverbanks (Cynthia Maas, 2010, B.C.), in creek beds (Cherisse Houle, 2009, Manitoba), in bags floating in rivers (Tina Fontaine, 2014, Saskatchewan). They are stabbed (Tara Chartrand, 2012, Saskatchewan), beaten to death (Amanda Jane Cook, 1996, Manitoba), struck on the head (Chelsey Acorn, 2005, B.C.), burned alive (Joyce Cardinal, 1993, Alberta), shot (Elisapi Assapa, 2003, Nunavut), drowned (Alacie Nowrakudluk, 1994, Quebec). Some families grieve the loss of two sisters

(Ginger and Deanna Bellerose, 2001 and 2002, Alberta); two cousins (Cecilia and Delphine Nikal, 1989 and 1990, B.C.);[12] an aunt and her niece (Glenda and Kelly Morriseau, 1991 and 2006, Manitoba and Quebec); a great-aunt and her great-niece (Tina Fontaine and Cheryl Duck, 2014 and 1988, Manitoba).[13]

Too often, nothing is left behind. No trace, no body (Maisy Odjick and Shannon Alexander, 2008, Quebec). Just a question mark that bores deep into the hearts of mothers, fathers, brothers, sisters and cousins. Families wrestle with the loss, investigate in the police's stead, protest at the little attention paid to them, but it's as though their cries are absorbed by a softly padded Canada resigned to the sorry lot of Indigenous peoples.

Silence.

For the longest time, the country harboured the delusion that this was nothing more than a series of random events occuring in self-imploding communities. Amnesty International turned that idea on its head in 2004 with its report titled *Stolen Sisters*. "It was undeniably a tragedy," I was told by Craig Benjamin, a campaigner for Indigenous rights with Amnesty. "But was it a human rights issue? Our conclusion is that it was. We could individualize each murder or murderer, but the issue was much broader than that, and the government failed to take appropriate measures."

* * *

"Did you and Maisy ever talk politics?"

Laurie gave her joyful booming laugh. On this cold mist-filled winter morning, it was bacon and beans for her, pancakes and maple syrup for me. We talked with our mouths full and the waitresses interrupted us every few minutes to refill Laurie's coffee cup. A report on Tricia Boisvert, a murdered Indigenous woman, was playing on the restaurant's TV screen. Her body had just been found in the region.

"Politics? No. Maisy was focused on herself, like all teens. Me, me, me." (Laurie's laugh again.) "But she was aware . . ."

"Of the situation of Indigenous peoples, reserves . . . ?"

"Of course. But we didn't get into politics. Me, I was never really involved before she went missing."

*
* *
*

I like the English word *empowerment*. Listening to these Indigenous mothers take the political class to task, in general, and, in particular, the prime minister, notoriously indifferent to their cause; seeing Laurie, known for her strength of character and eloquence, hold press conferences, help the families of missing women during gatherings, speak in front of the prime minister or the International Human Rights Commission in Washington, it's the word *empowerment* that comes to mind. Something that says: "I'm not afraid anymore. I'm going to fight because no one else will fight for me."

"I'd heard about the missing women, but I never thought one day I'd end up on the Hill with a picture of my daughter . . . I never thought that would be me. I've seen pictures on the Hill, you know . . . mothers with pictures of their missing daughters . . . And now . . . here I am."

Maisy gone has made of her mother a fighter. Laurie travels to Parliament Hill a couple of times a year, surrounded by members of her community. This October 4, like the others, Kitigan Zibi came out in force: its chief, the band council's female members, Bridget the activist, and community members who work with the NWAC in Ottawa. Pictures and videos of Laurie on the steps up to Parliament, all proof of her perseverance, year after year, with her husband Mark, sometimes with Bryan or Damon, her expression hardened or distraught, calling police to account, crying, "Shame on Canada! Shame on Canada for trying to bury another tragedy!"—an allusion to the residential schools.

Never give up, never back down, never forget, never keep quiet, never give in, never let anyone else speak on your behalf: *empowerment*.

6
INSIDE GIANT TIGER
August 2008

Late that summer of 2008, with school fast approaching—Maisy was to attend Maniwaki's adult education centre to work on her high school diploma after her year off; Shannon, Mont-Laurier's nursing school—both girls decided to cut their hair. Did they consult each other? Was it one of those twin impulses common to young teen friendships? Their pixie cuts appear in an *Ottawa Citizen* article: Maisy, a wisp of hair falling over one eye, an eyebrow raised, a wry look; Shannon smiling in the sunlight, her plucked eyebrows. Their grandmothers remember.

"Shannon always wore her hair long, but she said if she was going to be in school, if she was going to be studying, she didn't want to have to worry about her hair. So she got this short haircut and she was so pretty," Pam said.

"I used to work as a hairdresser, but I developed an allergy to the products we used for perms," Lisa told me.

"When we got back from Family Day, the annual picnic on the lakeshore, Maisy asked me to give her a haircut. She wanted to get rid of her thick long hair before school started. She said all that hair gave her a headache. Look at this picture!"

The shot was probably from August 30, 2008. A day or two earlier, Lisa drove Maisy to the agricultural fair in Shawville, not far from the Ontario border, two hours away; I could imagine tall Maisy and her Little Grandma strolling through the grounds, sitting in on the horse show, the poultry judging contest or the demolition derby; walking by the farm machinery, cows and steers.

"On our way back from Shawville, we stopped to shop for clothes at Giant Tiger," she continued.

Giant Tiger on Maniwaki's main street—one of those starkly lit warehouse stores that sells inexpensive clothing. Lisa offered Maisy "pants, a pair of shorts, a skirt, tights and a short sweater." She remembered everything. "So she'd have a wardrobe for school," she added. "We bumped into Shannon inside."

One winter day, I stopped in at Giant Tiger for gloves and socks. I asked the cashier if she knew the story of Shannon and Maisy; yes, of course, those two young girls who went missing, she replied. I felt like saying, then *did* say, that the girls had spoken to each other here, between the racks, just a few days before they disappeared. Oh,

said the cashier. I imagined Shannon and Maisy looking in the mirror, craning their necks to see a skirt from
the back. I wanted to revive their memory. I wanted the
salesclerks to remember them.

Giant Tiger, the store where Shannon and Maisy bought their clothes.

Looking back, Lisa thought that it was only then, just
a week before September 6, 2008, that she realized how
tightly knit the girls had become. Their close friendship
seemed to have developed without anyone noticing,
other than Bryan, who said he saw Maisy every day for
six months. The Kitigan Zibi police department, and the
retired officers volunteering for the Missing Children
Society of Canada, had their work cut out for them
gathering information on the girls' activities, even from

other young people their age. *Ottawa Citizen* journalist Brendan Kennedy did write, however, about Maisy: "Friends say the summer before Maisy disappeared appeared difficult for the teen . . . . [Her friend] M. said Maisy had drifted from some of her closest friends. She was moodier. There were rumours she was into harder drugs."[1] That speculation was never borne out.

*
*   *
*

Over the months, I realized that looking for a cause for their disappearance (for example, having fallen in with the wrong crowd through drug use) ventured into delicate political terrain. For years, activists have been fighting the police line claiming that young Indigenous women indulge in "at-risk behaviour": hitchhiking, drug abuse, homelessness, prostitution. Another term has met with the approval of Indigenous women's organizations. The term "vulnerability." Instead of implicitly levelling a reproach at these women—the missing, the dead—for opting for an at-risk lifestyle and suffering the consequences, the suggestion is that their lifestyle was not a choice but the product of social and historical fragility. Of course, the concept of "at-risk behaviour" has been useful for the police. Working with provincial police, the RCMP has created special task forces to shed light on the murders and disappearances of sex workers in Prairie cities and towns, and of hitchhikers along the Highway of Tears. But the propagation of that terminology leads the media to associate the deaths of Indigenous women with at-risk behaviour and, above all, with the sex trade, even when that is just not the case—80 percent of missing and murdered Indigenous women, as identified by researcher Maryanne Pearce, were not involved in sex work.

That approach has long criminalized victims and made it possible to ignore both the roots of the evil and the situation of close to 700,000 Indigenous—First Nations, Inuit, and Métis—women compared to that of other women in Canada. Their life expectancy is five to ten years shorter. Their income 30 percent lower. Twice as many are single parents; twice as many unemployed. Three times as many are victims of domestic abuse; three times as many likely to contract AIDS. They are four times more likely to become pregnant between the ages of fifteen and nineteen; five times more likely to live in overcrowded housing; seven times more likely to be murdered.

There are eight times more violent crimes on reserves than elsewhere in the country. But the violence affects Indigenous women living off reserve, a majority, just as much as those living on reserve.[2]

Vulnerable wherever they are. Vulnerable both in their communities—some of which have no clean drinking water and inadequate housing attacked by rot and mould, and are plagued by genuine epidemics of youth suicides,[3] showcasing devastation matched only in the Third World—and in the poorest districts of large cities.

*
* *
*

For the longest time, I thought there was a need to differentiate between spousal, family and community violence and "external" violence—sexual predators, serial killers, drug traffickers, pimps and street gangs; that is, that social violence and racial violence were separate. I was wrong. It's a continuum. One snowy morning in March 2014, I received an email from Val Napoleon, a professor at the University of Victoria in B.C. Ten years earlier, a research project had taken her to reserves bordering the Highway of Tears, a road she regularly travelled.

> *Just outside of the city limits of Prince George, to my horror, I saw two young Indigenous women hitchhiking. I pulled over to pick them up and when they were in the car, I said, "Don't you know that this is called the Highway of Tears? It is too dangerous to be hitchhiking along here!" They both looked at me, young faces. One had a world-weary air, the other was shy and quiet. The world-weary one, let's call her Ronnie, explained to me that she was a very experienced hitchhiker, had been hitchhiking for years. She knew all the truckers and they knew her. She knew the roads and knew how to stay safe. The two of them were hitchhiking from Vancouver to their home community in northwest B.C.—they*

had already been on the road for a couple of days. She said that her friend, the shy one, let's call her Ella, was new to hitchhiking so Ronnie was helping her get home, keeping an eye out for her. Ella had family business to attend to but they had no money to get there. Then Ronnie said, "And anyway, it is safer to hitchhike than it is to stay in our community. That is where it is really dangerous for us. We will head back to Vancouver after Ella is done." And we drove some hours and some hundreds of miles. When I stopped, they got out of the car and headed off on their journey. And there was nothing to say because my heart was too heavy.

So violence and poverty had forced "Ronnie" and "Ella" to leave their community for the big city hundreds of kilometres to the south. They likely eked out a living somehow in Vancouver, maybe in the Downtown Eastside. And they felt safer on the Highway of Tears, a graveyard for Indigenous hitchhikers, than on their reserve in northwestern B.C.

Now that is vulnerability's downward spiral.

Indigenous women's associations also refer to a vicious cycle. "Without housing or nearby women's shelters (as a case in point, there are only eleven shelters for fifty-two Quebec Indigenous communities), women and girls living in abusive situations often have nowhere to go," explained Alana Boileau, Justice and Public Safety

Coordinator for Quebec Native Women (QNW). "Afraid of being reported and having their children taken away unjustly by social services, often women don't press charges. If their children are placed in foster homes, women are given little time or assistance to improve their situation before losing their children permanently. When a woman is already dealing with problems of drug and alcohol abuse, losing her children only aggravates the situation."[4] The next stage can sometimes be for them to flee to the city, where they're at the mercy of predators. Each stage makes a woman more fragile, more easily hurt, raped, killed. Vulnerability begets vulnerability. Mental resources dwindle. The body ceases to matter. Death lies in ambush. Inadequate welfare and media apathy add to her hyperfragility.

Indigenous women are not the only women affected, but they are overrepresented in this ashen, silent cohort.

Wisps of straw, brittle twigs, snowflakes, ephemeral, invisible.

*
* *
*

The RCMP report published in May 2014[5] suggests the type of environment—violent, a breeding ground for crime—in which the 1,017 missing and murdered Indigenous women lived between 1980 and 2012. More often than for non-Indigenous victims, the offences linked to the murders were related to sexual assaults. Many more killers of Indigenous women had already committed violent offenses or consumed drugs or alcohol at the time of the crime. Of the Indigenous victims themselves, 63 percent had consumed alcohol and/or drugs before dying, compared to 20 percent of non-Indigenous victims. The report also showed that, by the time of their deaths, 18 percent had turned to illegal means to meet their basic needs, compared to 8 percent of other female homicide victims.

Little by little, with every report and disclosure, what had seemed obscure became clear. The RCMP report revealed that, as in the case of murdered women on average, 90 percent of the killers of Indigenous women were known to their victims. So it is the overrepresentation of Indigenous women and their numbers that are horrifying, even more than the circumstances of their murders.

The RCMP report reveals a crucial aspect: Indigenous women die first and foremost because they live in poor, violent districts. This is what can be gathered from the troubling numbers: compared to non-Indigenous victims, they are more often murdered by "acquaintances" (30 percent for Indigenous women, 19 percent for non-Indigenous women). "Acquaintances" are "close friends, neighbours, authority figures, business relationships, criminal relationships or casual acquaintances," according to the RCMP definition. This is not counting spouses or former spouses.[6] All of which points to the fact that these women are surrounded by violent men, both at home, clearly, and in their neighbourhoods. A situation striking in its singularity. Their killers are

Indigenous to be sure (particularly on reserves), but also non-Indigenous (in urban areas). And this violence, which can seem social in nature, has its origins in the racial violence perpetrated on Canada's First Nations since the sixteenth century.

I came to see Indigenous identity as being both a vulnerability factor—on the same level as living in a violent environment or being homeless or drug-addicted—and the very cause of every vulnerability.

*
*   *
*

Maisy and Shannon, well loved and happy, had clearly started down that path. They were walking the same tightrope. Maisy, the dropout, the rebel, still had a strong family backing her. Shannon bore the burden of struggling parents and a chaotic childhood, but her father adored her. Both of them taken at the top of that slippery slope; mowed down during their teenage rebellion—drinking, smoking, dyeing their hair blue, sleeping all day; falling off the tightrope just as they prepared to return to school.

"Shannon was thrilled to get into Mont-Laurier," Pam remembered. "She said, 'Grandma, Grandma, I was accepted. Grandma! I got in!' School started in October. So I gave Bryan the money so he could buy her what she needed. He bought her some clothes. He bought her a new suitcase. He bought her a computer and computer case. He bought her a cell phone."

That was the last thing Pam was able to do for Shannon. All those possessions bearing the promise of a new life, that spoke of a young girl's hope to escape her parents' fate and expressed her desire to leave the small town behind, shorn hair, light and free, all those possessions stayed behind in her apartment the night she disappeared.

7
Sept-Îles
March 20, 2014

Michèle Audette was the president of NWAC.[1] The daughter of an Innu woman from the North Shore and a Québécois man, she is the mother of five children, a long-time activist for the cause of Indigenous women and a former deputy minister with Quebec's Status of Women Secretariat; beautiful, bright, unpredictable. She divides her time between Ottawa and Uashat-Maliotenam, her community.

"Tell me, if you were made prime minister of Canada, what's the first thing you would do for Indigenous women?"

Michèle was in Sept-Îles, the city bordering the Uashat reserve, buying contact lenses. She was talking to me on her cell phone to me, interrupted periodically by the salesclerk. We clicked immediately, despite the hundreds of kilometres separating us, because of our shared obsessions.

"Three steps are needed, costly ones. First, an independent public inquiry into the murders and disappearances, more in-depth and exhaustive work than that done by parliamentary committees, an inquiry to be led by experts working with our association and families to identify all legislative, community and social gaps. There's no time to waste, we need to get this in place, then work on an action plan. The second step is to increase the number of shelters, transition housing and places for Indigenous women's social and economic reintegration. To start, you find protection from an abusive spouse, then you proceed to the next stage. Do you know the story of the Inuit woman who was murdered with her children by her husband just a few hours after being turned away from a shelter [Vivian Enuaraq, 2011, Quebec]? Outrageous. The third step is to heal our men of violence."

I'd thought Michèle Audette would be a woman who, for tactical reasons and because of who she was, would refuse to weigh in on Indigenous domestic abuse. I was wrong. She herself broached the subject from the outset, no holds barred. She dealt with the rest, too, telling me about the Inuit women who would come for treatment in the big cities to the south, only to be greeted at the airport by pimps promising the moon. She reminded me of the story of a mother in her thirties from Thunder Bay, Ontario, kidnapped, raped, beaten and left for dead in December 2012 by two white men who, the victim said, hurled their racism and hatred at her for the treaties and rights granted to Indigenous communities.

Michèle remembered the Harper government's radio silence after that attack, in contrast to the speed with which it spoke out against the horror of the gang rape in India that was making headlines worldwide at around the same time.

*
*   *
*

She spoke of momentum as well. It was her feeling that, finally, the interminable winter was giving way to something like fury, something like action. The wind had picked up. We watched as four women from Saskatchewan founded the Indigenous social movement "Idle No More," one of the most important social movements in North America, speaking out not only against the Harper government's new anti-environment legislation but also against the compromises made by Indigenous powers-that-be with the federal authority characterized as colonial; we watched as Mi'kmaq women from New Brunswick and Innu women from Quebec blockaded roads to protest the exploitation of natural resources near their communities, women wearing traditional skirts and beating their drums, sometimes against the wishes of their own band councils or husbands, more inclined to negotiate.

We watched as the chief of an isolated reserve in northern Ontario went on a hunger strike in a tipi erected just a stone's throw from the prime minister's offices to denounce living conditions in her community.

Each and every demand included the need to bring an end to violence against Indigenous women, whether it came from large grant-receiving Indigenous organization such as the Assembly of First Nations (AFN) or from grassroots movements. Everything seemed inextricably linked: the disdain shown by the government and the oil and gas industry toward First Nations' treaties and lands; the ineffectiveness, dilution, inadequacy and at times insufficiency of federal subsidies purportedly designed to provide support to reserves; the social and psychological breakdown of communities and the vicious cycles that led to violence against women. Indigenous intellectuals—Lee Maracle, Leanne Simpson and Andrea Landry, to name but a few—wrote, railed, conceptualized, theorized, linking the attacks against women's bodies to attacks against First Nations' lands.[2] I discovered a distinct Indigenous feminism, unfettered, radical, founded on the idea of decolonization and a return to the gender equity that had prevailed among First Nations before the game-changing arrival of Europeans five hundred years earlier.

Momentum, she said. The year 2013 was marked by warnings, reports and wake-up calls sent to the Harper government around the #MMIW tragedy. The non-governmental organization Human Rights Watch (HRW) made public a damning report on the RCMP's treatment of Indigenous women in northern B.C.— at issue were failings, serious neglect and even violence perpetrated by police against women.[3] The

Oppal Commission on Missing Women in Vancouver's Downtown Eastside published a report, *Forsaken*, condemning mistakes made by the police investigation, specifically attributing them to the investigators' racism, whether conscious or unconscious. Canada's provincial and territorial premiers called for a public and national inquiry. The Inter-American Commission on Human Rights sent a team to investigate the issue during the summer of 2013. The United Nations Human Rights Council urged Canada to carry out a "national review." As James Anaya, UN special rapporteur for the rights of Indigenous peoples, travelled through Canada, he expressed alarm at the "disturbing phenomenon of aboriginal women missing and murdered at the hands of both aboriginal and non-aboriginal assailants, whose cases have a much higher tendency to remain unsolved than those involving non-aboriginal victims."[4] All in the same year. And the federal government's reaction? Like a citadel under siege convinced it was in the right, the government rejected the UN Human Rights Council's call to action, claiming that certain signatories—Cuba, Iran, Russia—were far from human rights exemplars themselves.[5] The government dug in its heels, offering its detractors measures that were either already in place or in the process of being implemented—the National Police Support Centre for Missing Persons,[6] the improvement of women's matrimonial status on reserves, the delivery of pamphlets on "the importance of reducing the intergenerational cycle of violence," the collection and dissemination of Indigenous groups' best practices to improve women's safety, and $25 million over five years designed to put an end to community violence.

* *
*

Momentum. The murder of Loretta Saunders in February 2014 became the subject of heated debate in the House of Commons and triggered a series of radical articles on Indigenous and feminist Indigenous blogs. Loretta was twenty-six and three months pregnant. She was of Inuit heritage and studying at St. Mary's University in Halifax, 2,000 km from her small hometown in Labrador. The subject of the thesis she was working on was missing and murdered Indigenous women. Police believe she was killed on February 13, the very day a 23,000-name petition calling for a national inquiry was delivered and the day before annual countrywide commemorative marches took place.

The symbolism defies the imagination.

But Loretta, born of an Inuit mother and a Métis father, had wheat blond hair, blue eyes and the striking features of a Hollywood WASP icon. Her two roommates and presumed killers, a young marginal couple with a turbulent past, allegedly killed her when she asked them for their share of the rent. For several weeks, I thought the terrible tragedy had no link to the Indigenous issue; I and others had our doubts about the way it was being brandished. Then I discovered that Loretta had left her family at the age of fifteen and spent several years (several years!) on the streets of Montreal—no one knows under what living conditions, other than that she sometimes found herself in "very scary situations" as recounted by her sister[7]—and that she eventually returned to Labrador, gaunt and exhausted. So, despite the colour of her eyes and her freckles, despite having a loving family so stable that it also fostered other children, despite all that, Loretta had inherited the malaise that runs through Indigenous generations and communities. Amazingly resilient, even while still battling a drug addiction, she upgraded her skills enough to attend university, where she became an outstanding student.[8] She told her family how much she identified with the subject of her thesis. "She saw herself in the statistics. She saw me," her sister reported. "She saw the girls we grew up with." Short of money, she chose to share her apartment with two near-strangers: this is a recurring theme in families' accounts: the blind trust that vulnerable girls placed in the people whose paths they crossed. So much so that the murder of blonde Loretta is a reflection of inherited vulnerability and, in activists' eyes, a prime example of the ongoing tragedy. Her murder also shows that a rise to success or to the premises of social success does not offer protection—or not always.

Her body was found along the TransCanada highway in New Brunswick thirteen days after she went missing, in a snow-covered hockey bag.[9] A hashtag sprang up on activist sites and social media: *#ItEndsHere*.

Three weeks later a highly anticipated parliamentary report was released, *Invisible Women: A Call to
Action*. Liberal MPs had wrested from the Conservative
majority the creation of a special committee on violence
against Indigenous women which, over an eleven-month
period, heard from NGOs and Indigenous organizations,
police, community groups, social workers, researchers,
senior civil servants and families from across the country. Amnesty International participated. As did Bridget
Tolley of Kitigan Zibi Anishinabeg and the Families
of Sisters in Spirit. As did Connie Greyeyes. Michèle
Audette. And so many others. But not Laurie.

"I was asked to go," she pointed out. "I don't believe
in that committee; I refused to go there. A committee headed up by a Conservative, with a majority of
Conservative MP members. Give me a break!" Laurie had
already met Stephen Harper in Ottawa circa 2010, she
doesn't remember the exact date. At a meeting organized
by the Missing Children Society of Canada with other
families of missing children, she had to tell him her story
in less than three minutes and remembered his coldness
and his blatant desire to be anywhere but there. To this
day, she hopes for nothing from the Conservatives, other
than to see them leave office.

What was to come proved Laurie right. The report
was both fair and disturbing, but its recommendations were entirely trivial, making for a schizophrenic
whole. Other than two resolutions—the creation of a
national genetic data inventory of missing persons and

the potential of having police gather data on violence against women that would take their ethnic origin into account—the commitments did nothing more than perpetuate existing policies. Once again, the government refused outright to hold a national public inquiry of any kind. Once again, the Conservatives put off a face-to-face encounter both with Canada's colonial history and with the segment of its population that persists in tarnishing the country's image, upsetting the UN and spoiling the fun.

From the start, people suspected the government was up to its tricks with the committee, and anger often erupted in the hearing room. Speaking from Uashat, Michèle Audette voiced her exasperation: "Let me be clear. We've reached the end of our rope. I realize [the committee] is the only instrument available to us right now, but I've been in politics for twenty years now, first representing Quebec's Indigenous women and now the NWAC, and this is not the first nor, I fear, the last time we will find ourselves in this position, waiting and hoping, with our recommendations in hand. But most of the time, let's be realistic . . . our recommendations are relegated to a shelf somewhere to gather dust."[10] For her part, the committee's vice-president, Carolyn Bennett, a Liberal, publicly criticized both the scant amount of time devoted to the families and the mediocrity of the approach adopted in drafting the report, which clearly revealed a desire not to rock the boat; in her view, the committee and its report were "a total travesty of

Parliamentary process."[11] Putting her money where her mouth was, Michèle Audette, who had threatened during the hearings to jump into the political arena, announced in May that she would be running as a Liberal during the next election. That very day, the RCMP announced the release of the most detailed report on the topic to date. Momentum indeed.

In September 2014, bowing to strong media pressure on the heels of Tina Fontaine's murder, the federal government made public an "action plan to respond to domestic violence and violent crimes against Indigenous girls and women." In reality, it was simply an update of the $25-million five-year plan announced seven months earlier. The new iteration emphasized family support, but remained silent as to the deep-rooted causes of the tragedy: poverty, the lack of a sufficient number of foster homes, a more vigilant police force. The principle of a large-scale public inquiry was once again shelved.

Indigenous activists and organizations continue to debate the relevance of such a public inquiry. "If the colonial government were to put dollars into 'fixing' an issue they continuously create and justify, and if we were to agree to work with them, it would be like shaking hands with and embodying the oppressor,"[12] writes Andrea Landry. We are our own experts, say Landry and other women who, like her, call for sovereignty, self-determination. "We must come up with the solutions ourselves," they write.

But the Indigenous world does come together in

rejecting the Conservative government. Which responds in kind. In the special committee's final report, I came across a small yet significant instance of censorship. On October 4, 2013, when Connie Greyeyes spoke on Parliament Hill of the eleven deaths and disappearances in her close circle, she ended with a poem by Helen Knott, a young Indigenous activist, dedicated to Indigenous murder victims. The poem ends with these lines:

> *Finally, given the stars,*
> *laid to gaze at them on back roads*
> *and in ditches,*
> *on ghostly stretches*
> *forgotten pebbled pathways.*
> *Your vastness*
> *swallows me.*
> *Do I fall in your line of sight?*
> *Do you see me now, Stephen Harper?*
> *Because it feels to me*
> *like your eyes*
> *curve*
> *around me.*[13]

Connie also read the entire poem to the committee during the family hearing on December 9. The final report, *Invisible Women*, begins in fact with that text. But its "Do you see me now" is followed by a question mark.

The prime minister's name has disappeared.

8
POLICE STATION, KITIGAN ZIBI
January 24, 2014

Kitigan Zibi is laid out in an unnerving way, with no true centre, no circularity. Its administration, daycare, handicrafts store, general store—where Laurie's husband works—extend down either side of Highway 105, while the bankrupt Home Hardware, whose signage then logo disappeared over the course of my visits, still exists on residents' mental map. The building's picture can still be seen on the reserve's website; it's easy to imagine what an important source of employment it must have been, and community members continue to designate the "Home Hardware parking lot" as a meeting spot, as if the former store were an amputated leg whose contours can still be felt. Close to Highway 105, a small street with its white church hints at what the community must have looked like fifty or a hundred years ago—rustic, close-knit. But now one crosses from Kitigan Zibi to Maniwaki, from the Indigenous reserve to the white town, with no warning.

The now-closed Home Hardware was a hub of community life. Laurie
was at work there when she heard of Maisy's disappearance.

To the west lies a beautiful wilderness area, lakes
too numerous to count, an uninterrupted forest where
houses spring up every half kilometre or so, as though
in an attempt to occupy the land while recognizing their
smallness in that huge expanse. I dubbed this area "the
roads-without-end sector," although they call them
streets, *mikan* in Algonquin. That's where Laurie and
Lisa live, ten kilometres apart.

The frustrating, fragmented geography is under-
standable when you realize how Algonquin territory
has been gradually whittled away as logging operations
invade the region. "We've been losing ground, losing
ground, retreating, retreating," the community's chief,
Gilbert Whiteduck, told me. "See the Maniwaki shopping
centre over there, by the river? That's where our chief
Pakinawatik had his home in the nineteenth century."
Gilbert acknowledged that landscapes change and urban

centres evolve, but in this case, territory was being confiscated and promises broken.

In 2012, Kitigan Zibi's band council listed twenty-three land claims involving Maniwaki land. The reserve has lost 5,000 hectares since its creation in 1851 and, as Gilbert pointed out, many of the lands were removed outside the scope of any treaty or accord: they were stolen.

The police station is located on Kikinamage Street, where the school, the community radio station, social and health services and the women's shelter are found as well. In the heart of the reserve, far from the administrative centre and Highway 105. I drove one night through the snow and got lost; eventually I arrived in front of the small brick building where Gordon McGregor, police chief in charge of eight officers, was waiting for me. That's a lot of officers for a community of 1,600, yet not enough if you take into account all the problems facing reserves. I thought he would be big, strong, calm; he was big, strong and calm. He has been an officer in Kitigan Zibi for thirty-two years, and chief of police for twenty-two. "How do you do it?" I asked him. "You've known everyone for so long, it must be hard to stay detached." The untenable situation of Indigenous police officers, who are born and raised in the community they work in, had been described to me—how they end up having to intervene in the case of a cousin selling drugs or an aunt beaten by her husband.

"Living so close is unusual," he agreed. "You arrest youngsters whose parents you know. Fathers come to my house to knock at the door and say, 'What can I do for my son?' It's impossible for me to just be the police chief. People speak to me as to an elder; they come to me for advice."

"All the same . . . you can't be God," I said.

"I'm not God, but I'm there. I can't send people back to their homes, I have to hear them out. I just ask my girlfriend, 'Please, go upstairs,' or we leave the room. If you turn them away, they won't tell you anything anymore or share information with you. So I'm available, always available; it's rare for me to go away. It's a double-edged sword. Even offenders on the other side of the fence respect me. In thirty years, I've only been punched once."

"What keeps you busy right now?"

"You mean," he smiled, "what's the flavour of the month?"

He ran through the list of concerns from the past few years: marijuana and cocaine trafficking with the U.S. in 2006 and 2007; then the illegal trafficking of prescription drugs between 2008 and 2010.

"At the time, there were a lot of thefts and fatal overdoses. We lost three or four kids from those pills. Now we deal with the mental health issues that come from that period. There are a lot of people that are still trying to recover from that time, years after."

The Kitigan Zibi police station.

In 2005, Gordon was accused of using a police credit card to pay for salsa lessons with his girlfriend at Maniwaki's upscale hotel. The accusers were drug traffickers from the reserve who knew they were under surveillance. Gordon was cleared by Quebec's police ethics committee and helped arrest a dozen community members.

In April 2008, on a different note entirely, he managed to capture a lion cub called Boomer, which had been kept illegally on the reserve and had escaped, making front-page news in Ontario and Quebec. Pictures show him, a good-looking man, moustache, white shirt, smiling calmly, surrounded by his men, coaxing the little lion cub into the police station. On September 6 of that same year, Maisy and Shannon's disappearance put Gordon front and centre again. More accurately, it put him in the hot seat.

*
* *
*

By September 2008, Bryan and his daughter Shannon had lived for four years in social housing on Koko Street in Maniwaki, only a few dozen metres from the reserve. "Straight on the line," explained Gordon, meaning the boundary. Maisy came to stay on the weekend of September 6 and 7. It was in that apartment that the girls were seen for the last time, by Bryan. Although both girls disappeared from the same place at the same time, two different police forces became involved: the reserve police took over Maisy's file, and the Maniwaki police detachment, the Sûreté du Québec (SQ), took over Shannon's. In the days following the missing persons report, both teams visited Bryan's apartment, without any coordination whatsoever, whisking away some clues, perhaps trampling others.

A little over six months after the young girls' disappearance, Montreal's Missing Justice Association website published an open letter from Laurie, bitter and filled with dismay.

> *I feel as though I do not have the right to exercise my right to information concerning my minor daughter. For instance, when I called*

*the Sûreté du Québec to speak to a police offi-
cer investigating the Shannon Alexander case,
I was told to speak to the Kitigan Zibi police
services because la Sûreté does not have my file,
and I am not related to Shannon. I understand
the need for confidentiality; however, where else
can I turn for police information when in fact I
receive next to no information from the KZPS.
And, when I do receive any information from
the KZPS, it is just snippets and unprofessional
in nature. . . . **WHY WAS MY DAUGHTER'S
FILE TRANSFERRED TO THE KITIGAN
ZIBI POLICE SERVICES BY THE SÛRETÉ
DU QUÉBEC? WHO GAVE THIS ORDER?** . . .
The disappearance happened while she was off
reserve, therefore, the Sûreté du Québec is the
proper police force to conduct the investigation
and handle the case. I do not wish for my daughter to become a jurisdictional issue.*[1]

Cooperation between the two departments was
required; the alleged crime could just as easily have
taken place on reserve land as in Maniwaki. But no
investigator had been designated as the lead. Disorga-
nization and a lack of strategy seemed to reign supreme.
After six months, there was little to show for the
police's efforts because they failed to take advantage of
the first days after the disappearance. Those two deci-
sive weeks, during which valid clues could have been

gathered and accounts taken from witnesses while still fresh in their mind, had been wasted because of a poor division of roles. When questioned by a journalist from the *Ottawa Citizen,* both forces explained that, "during the first two months of the investigation . . . the cases were being handled separately."[2] Mark and Laurie were never questioned ("As Maisy's stepfather, shouldn't I have been a suspect?" Mark observed). Having been on the front line, Bryan was questioned, but he was cleared. Once the girls' pictures were broadcast over the media beginning in mid-September, the police departments seemed to be overwhelmed by all the (false) leads they followed up on. "It's like a computer overloaded; it all scrambles after a while," Gordon explained.[3]

However, speaking to me in the small police station, he waved away any suggestion of inefficiencies due to the dual investigation. In his view, what they lacked in September 2008 played a much more important role: resources and expertise, both within his police department and in the SQ. Not enough manpower, not enough skills. He repeated it like a mantra. "Tracking down a missing person is a specialist's job. In drug investigations, you have to keep everything confidential so you can arrest the person trafficking. But here, it was a whole different approach that we weren't used to. We were looking at a public investigation to get new leads, and we wondered, 'What can I tell this person, how far can I go?'"

In March 2009, after months of insistence, Laurie

finally received a document from the Kitigan Zibi police
department, which she refers to in her open letter:

> *Just recently, I received an eight-page double-*
> *spaced document with no letterhead or signa-*
> *ture. I have to point out that after reading the*
> *document, I felt like I had been doing the police's*
> *job for it because all I found were the clues and*
> *sources I myself had provided. All in all, nothing*
> *solid. Once again, I end up with even more ques-*
> *tions, doubts and a feeling of an utter emptiness.*

The report, which covered the period from September
to December 2008, listed off the information gathered,
searches done (on Quebec and Ontario reserves nearby,
in an abandoned house, along the railway tracks next to
Kitigan Zibi), exchanges with the SQ, and missing persons bulletins broadcast as far as the U.S. border. All kinds
of sightings of the girls had been reported since their disappearance: in the neighbouring towns of Messines and
Déléage; on several Ottawa streets, by the Tim Hortons
in Vanier, Ottawa's Indigenous district; hitchhiking
along the highway; in Gatineau, Quebec; in Kingston,
Hanover, Port Elgin; in Saugeen, Mark's reserve, which
Maisy missed so much; in an Owen Sound grocery store.
Local police had been contacted. Every time, the conclusion was the same: *No results.*

The investigation failed to make any headway. A

Maniwaki hockey coach, accused of raping a minor (the same man committed suicide in prison in 2011), became a suspect and was interrogated. Two young men from the community—including the young man Laurie picked up one day in her car—were questioned. In Gordon's view, "we had followed all possible leads, questioned all suspects, once, twice, three times. After the pictures were released, when reports of sightings came in from Ottawa or Kingston, we began working with the Ontario Provincial Police and the RCMP. No results." There was not just the boundary between the reserve and Maniwaki to consider; there was the border separating Quebec and Ontario as well. The probability of finding the girls on the Ontario side was greater: Shannon was born in Ottawa and her mother lives there; it is the big city for people living in the Outaouais region. Plus, Maisy had lived in Ontario for several years, in Saugeen; she had also spent time at her father's place in the same province on the Six Nations reserve. So four police departments were involved in the investigation, without any one in particular heading up the coordination or organizing the searches.

During that whole time, basic clues had not been gathered. Or only poorly so, Bryan maintained, describing a visit he received from the SQ. "They found a dried blood stain on the floor. Yeah, there were cats and dogs in the house, it could have been theirs, but I showed it to the police and said, 'There's dried blood here.' You know what they did? They asked me for a Q-tip and a piece of paper. I went to get a Q-tip and tore a piece of paper off an old colouring book of Shannon's. They put a bit of water on the Q-tip, took a sample of the stain and wrapped the Q-tip in the piece of paper. I stared at them and thought to myself, 'This is bullshit!' It was contaminated. They should have sealed everything."

Bryan told me how badly the few visits he had from the SQ had gone, describing how a young officer searching Shannon's bedroom had smiled as he held between his fingers a pair of her panties bearing a humorous inscription. Often drunk, in the pit of despair, Bryan made things even harder, threatening them and shouting at them.

Was Bryan right in what he said, given his freely admitted drinking and smoking, especially intense during those days of despair? His story is specific, detailed. I would have liked the SQ to corroborate or refute his story, but "no comment on ongoing cases" was the only answer I was given.

As for Laurie and Lisa, they were at odds with the Kitigan Zibi police investigator in charge of Maisy's file. Who, the two women claim, never answered their phone calls. "Why don't you ever call me, why don't you give me any news?" Laurie complained. "It's up to you to call us," he retorted. Lisa also complained of the official silence. "Let us do our fucking job," she was told. Several months later, Gordon acknowledged to *Ottawa Citizen* reporter Brendan Kennedy that the police "look into every bit of information that comes in, but they are not actively looking for the girls."[4]

In 2013, testifying at the special committee, Bridget Tolley, the co-founder of Sisters in Spirit and a resident of Kitigan Zibi, expressed her indignation. "We have two missing girls from 2008 and still they're not found. We lost a little baby lion on the reserve. We had a search party. We had the police. We had helicopters. We had game wardens. We had everything. When these two human beings went missing, we had nothing. There were no dogs, no search party, no police, no media . . . " No police-organized search, that's true, although the investigators were present during the searches organized by the families. No helicopter to fly over the area. When the girls' pictures were re-released to the media in September 2009, the Ontario Provincial Police organized an Ottawa press conference without advising the families. Alerted by a CBC journalist, Laurie raced from Kitigan Zibi, aghast, convinced that her public criticism of the investigation was behind the "oversight." The *Ottawa Citizen* journalist wrote: "Laurie Odjick, mother of Maisy Odjick, said she hasn't heard from police in about eight months. 'So, [as] for them saying they've been collaborating with the families—they haven't been talking to me.'"[5]

The relationship was officially over. For the Odjick family, the reserve's police department was incompetent and quick to lay blame.

> *To me it feels like the KZPS and Kitigan Zibi fell back on blaming the victim. I'm the victim, but*

for the authorities, this is all my fault if Maisy
left; it's my fault if she went missing; I'm the one
who waited too long to report her disappearance
to the police; I'm the one who didn't contact the
investigators on a regular basis.[6]

The Alexander family felt neglected and scorned by the SQ. "Because we're Indians," said Shannon's grandmother Pam, "that's why they treat us this way."

Pam, whom one might expect to be cautious, "assimilated," having worked for so many years for the Canadian army.

From the start, a bias existed. A bias behind the sluggish investigation. And the police silence encountered by the families. Consistently brought up at each parliamentary inquiry or hearing on missing and murdered Indigenous women.

The bias involved the firmly rooted notion within both police departments that the girls had run away from home. That they would be back any week now. I had read that, on average, Indigenous teenagers were more likely than other teens to run away—and so the police deployed fewer measures to find these girls despite the particularly worrying aspects surrounding this particular disappearance.[7]

Gordon McGregor acknowledged as much. "Yes,

that's the first thing I thought. I didn't know Shannon, but I knew Maisy had already run away. She was mad at her mother. I know that Maisy never got used to being back in Kitigan Zibi after her years in Saugeen." The report described by Laurie and written by the reserve investigator adopted the same angle. There had been long phone calls to Saugeen from Bryan's apartment, and several friends mentioned Maisy's desire to move back there; one friend even said Maisy had specifically mentioned moving there because she didn't get along with her mother.

Gordon added, "We shared information back and forth with the SQ for a couple of weeks until we realized the situation was not a good situation. We saw that their running away made no sense."

It was too late. The clues had vanished.

When the girls' computers were seized, a month after they went missing, police found emails expressing their desire to strike out for new horizons. The officers took this as confirmation of their hypothesis, and the SQ in Maniwaki stood by that hypothesis for the longest time, even mentioning it publicly to journalists in March 2009. Despite hearing Laurie insist that her daughter wouldn't have run away because she'd already left home. "She'd already packed her bags. She moved in with her boyfriend, then her grandma. She was living her life." As for Shannon, she was off to live in Mont-Laurier.

Like Laurie, Bryan attributed the lax investigation, despite troubling clues, to that bias. "I went to my son's in Ottawa for a couple of days," Bryan told me. "When I came home at five on Sunday, the apartment was empty. Maisy's grandma called me the next day to say both girls [had gone] missing. I didn't believe it. She came over and we sat down on my couch to talk. That's where I found Maisy's wallet and a pipe for dope. Then we went into Shannon's room and I found Shannon's wallet . . . I thought, 'What the fuck?'"

Both of their wallets, ID, money, makeup, clothes: everything was still there. Everything left behind seemed glaring proof that the girls had not left voluntarily. "If you leave behind what matters most . . . those are what we call red flags, worrying signs, alarm bells," I was told by Maryanne Pearce, who analyzed numerous police investigations for her thesis. "They're cause for immediate concern. Every possible clue is important."

The runaway hypothesis, broadly relayed by the media, had left its mark.

"Especially on TV . . . that makes a major impact on families. I'm sure most of the community here believe that they still ran away," Laurie told me. "I get this sometimes. They ask, 'Did you hear from Maisy yet?' I don't get mad, I don't blame them, it's because of the media . . . I say, 'No, nothing yet . . .' but back in my head, I say 'GRRRR.'"

Laurie said this last bit with a laugh. Then Mark added, "It's easier to believe that they ran away, more than something happened in the community."

And even if they had run away. "We could have

looked for them, couldn't we?" cried Pam, Shannon's grandmother. "They were sixteen and seventeen!"

There is no doubt that the disappearance of two pretty young girls, had they been a bit blonder and fairer-skinned, even if they'd been a tad wild or suspected runaways, would have triggered a totally different search response. An abundance of resources. An orgy of police. You can imagine the outpouring. All the more so after what occurred a month later in Ontario when young Brandon Crisp, fifteen, ran away, slamming the door to his family home on October 18, 2008, because his parents had confiscated his Xbox.[8]

The disproportion is staggering.

No ground search was launched for Maisy and Shannon by police *because they thought the girls were runaways and so would eventually come home*; for Brandon, *who was in fact a confirmed runaway*, the ground search lasted two whole weeks, with infrared cameras, a helicopter and tracking dogs. Embarrassed by young Brandon's addiction to the video game *Call of Duty*, Microsoft, the Xbox manufacturer and the family's Internet provider, immediately offered a reward of $50,000 to anyone who could help find him, while it took months for Laurie and her former sister-in-law Maria Jacko to raise $20,000 through golf tournaments and races. Brandon died when he fell from a tree, and his body was found by hunters three weeks after his disappearance in a wilderness area several kilometres from his hometown, Barrie. In Quebec five months later, in

February 2009, David Fortin, a teenager from Alma, was also labelled a runaway by police when he disappeared.[9] But that didn't stop them from deploying a helicopter and organizing ground searches with tracking dogs. Even though he was never found. "I'm not happy for the outcome, of course," Laurie said about Brandon. "But I'm envious of the attention."

It wasn't just a matter of finding the girls. After all, the police didn't find Brandon in time and have never found David. In Maisy and Shannon's case, it was about feeling institutional support as well. When Maisy and Shannon disappeared, both the Ontario Provincial Police and the SQ kept their involvement to a minimum, only to bring out the big guns several weeks or months later for teenagers and families with whom they more readily identified. When the big guns were finally brought out in Kitigan Zibi and Maniwaki, it wasn't a police initiative. The same negligence is apparent in every report on missing and murdered Indigenous women.

Listening to Connie Greyeyes tell the special committee about the eleven women in her circle who had disappeared or been murdered, I felt like she was living in a war zone. Laurie Odjick and Bryan Alexander, faced with the same police negligence, also seemed to me to be living in a country other than Canada, in some developing, as yet unformed, banana republic. They live in the same province as I do, drive through the same countryside, shop at the same grocery stores, yet their view of the country must be so different, like living in a hostile, oppressive land (albeit the land of their ancestors); they suffer the bitterness of historic dispossession and feel the effects of successive waves of destruction targeting their culture, their language, their families.

There are myriad accounts of police discrimination, whether conscious or unconscious. Several are found in the special committee's report.[10]

Such as Lorna Martin, speaking of her missing mother (Marie Jeanne Saint Saveur, Alberta, 1987). "One of the first questions the RCMP asked my sister was if she [my mother] drank. Arlene couldn't deny it. She didn't lie. She said yes. He said, 'They go on a drinking binge for two or three days and then they come back.' . . . When you're full of anxiety, you're hurting, it feels like a kick in the stomach. . . . They said our mom was a drunken Indian." (Marie Jeanne Saint Saveur suffered from mental health problems as a result of a childhood spent in Indian residential schools. She was a fragile woman.)

Or such as Amy Miller, speaking of her murdered daughter (Denise Bourdeau, Ontario, 2007). "The night we reported Denise missing the one officer had the nerve to say to the other officer in front of Glen and me, 'She's probably downtown doing whatever she has to do to get her next fix.'" (Denise Bourdeau was neither a sex worker nor a drug addict. She was a victim of spousal abuse.)

Or such as Bernadette Smith, speaking of her missing sister (Claudette Osborne, Manitoba, 2008). "When my sister went missing, she was reported missing, but it was ten days before her case was even looked at. My other sister, Tina, was told that she was probably out there somewhere; that's what the police told us, that they weren't going to do anything right now, that she'd turn up, she always did." (Claudette, a sex worker and drug addict, still had close ties with her family and was in touch regularly. Her silence was a worrying sign.)

*
* *
*

"Systemic racism": the expression is used in study after study, report after report. In fact, major lapses in investigations by the Vancouver police department and the RCMP into disappearances in the Downtown Eastside were so shocking that they became the focus of a commission of inquiry. "Racism, apathy and blatant disdain for the marginalized women whose life circumstances were anathema to police management led to inaction. These women were not afforded the same protection before they disappeared and the same concern, time and resources after they had gone missing, that would have been afforded to citizens deemed more worthy,"[11] wrote Maryanne Pearce. Systemic racism exists, despite the special police squads set up by the RCMP, such as KARE in Alberta, which looks for the killers of a group of "at-risk" women killed in the Edmonton area, 63 percent of whom were Indigenous; E-PANA in B.C., which deals with murders and disappearances along the Highway of Tears, 75 percent of whose victims were Indigenous; DEVOTE in Manitoba, which follows up on the murders of "at-risk" women in Winnipeg: prostitutes, the homeless, drug addicts, 64 percent of whom were Indigenous.[12]

In its report titled *Those Who Take Us Away*[13]—the title a translation of an Indigenous term used during the residential school period and designating the RCMP (whose officers removed children from their families)— Human Rights Watch (HRW) accuses the RCMP in northern B.C. not only of ignoring Indigenous women who file complaints (of spousal abuse, for instance) but also of insulting and hitting them. One of the women interviewed by HRW, her anonymity guaranteed, declared that she was raped by four RCMP officers. "The threat of domestic and random violence on one side, and mistreatment by RCMP officers on the other, leaves indigenous women in a constant state of insecurity,"[14] stated Meghan Rhoad, a women's rights researcher with HRW. Vulnerable three times over. In 2004, still in B.C., Justice David Ramsay was found guilty of beating and forcing unprotected sex on four Indigenous prostitutes between the ages of twelve and sixteen, three of whom had cases in his docket. "Where men seek out women to abuse, Aboriginal women are seen to be an easy target and low risk. Additionally, societal racism and stereotypes held by police officers can create an atmosphere of mutual distrust and ineffectual investigations when Aboriginal women are abused, go missing or are murdered,"[15] Maryanne Pearce writes as well.

There was scarcely any doubt as to the ineffectiveness of investigations into the murder of Indigenous
women until May 2014, when the RCMP's numbers were
made public. The report is titled *Missing and Murdered
Aboriginal Women: A National Operational Overview,*
and the cover illustration shows, dream-like, a young
girl in a traditional jingle dress dancing in the middle of
a prairie. It could be mistaken for the annual report of
an NGO, given the desire for redemption and redress it
reveals. However, the logo above the picture of the young
Indigenous woman—a man on horseback holding a flag,
namely an exact replica of nineteenth-century images of
the Mounted Police—is a potent reminder of the extent
to which the RCMP served as a force for colonization in
Western Canada.

Besides providing data on killers and victims, the
report indicates the rate of solved cases, which contra-
dicts the inertia and disdain denounced by so many families, researchers and reports: the solve rate is said to
be 89 percent for homicides of non-Indigenous women
and 88 percent for Indigenous women. That rate seems
to give the lie to reports from HRW and the Oppal
Commission on police ineffectiveness, thus invalidating
the idea that killers of Indigenous women benefit from
impunity.

Could that be right? Could this be a lie or intention-
ally misleading?

What, for instance, were Maryanne Pearce's
thoughts on the matter? "What it comes down to is that

POLICE STATION, KITIGAN ZIBI

most of these unsolved cases are likely to be strangers." The 12 percent of unsolved homicides of Indigenous women are probably linked to murders committed by "strangers."

The logical deduction would then be that even if police had brought out the big guns, they would have had trouble identifying those 10 to 12 percent of killers. Police inertia might have been masked by the level of difficulty of the cases.

Craig Benjamin of Amnesty International sees things differently. "The clearance figure in the report is based on cases that the police have accepted are homicides," he specifies. "My biggest question is about the suspicious deaths that police failed to seriously investigate, ruling them accidental, and of course the long-term missing persons cases which may in fact be homicides (and which I do think the report underestimates because of an inability to resolve the failure to record Aboriginal identity in the original police files)."

In any event, this report does not show the number of investigations organized by the families themselves, hence facilitating police work. The parents of young mother Daleen Kay Bosse, who was murdered in 2004 in Saskatoon, paid $250,000 to a private detective once they saw the police's slipshod approach to their daughter's case. Once the killer was close to being identified, the RCMP hopped on the bandwagon.

Similarly, if Maisy and Shannon's disappearance is one day solved, any credit should go to Laurie, who fought hard so the case would not be pushed aside and forgotten. After the unfortunate handling of the file by the officer from Mont-Laurier, who, according to Laurie, disclosed the two suspects' names, an officer from the SQ's Department of Investigations into Crimes Against Persons took over the investigation and communicates regularly with Laurie.

As for Gordon, he found himself dealing with a new disappearance on the reserve in late October 2013.

*
* *
*

Could it have been a bad dream? Once again, two women from the community had gone missing, leaving behind their wallets and ID. In a staggering twist of fate, Laura, one of the missing women, is the daughter of Bridget Tolley, the activist who started the October 4 vigils and co-founded Families of Sisters in Spirit, which, year after year in Ottawa and day after day on social media, opens its arms to parents devastated by the death or disappearance of their daughters. This time, the reserve's administration and the police did bring out the big guns, investigating all over the place, organizing searches, bringing in a helicopter. The near-immediate media coverage of the twin disappearances from Kitigan Zibi was like a crowning achievement for Bridget's activism. But the missing woman was her daughter, a mother of four children including a three-month-old baby. A bitter victory indeed.

I was about to leave for Kitigan Zibi to attend the search when Laurie told me the young women had been found deep in the woods by Pythonga Lake, an hour's drive northwest of the reserve. They had been partying and drinking, and for some unknown reason ventured into the forest when their car died. They found refuge in a cabin and eventually left their shelter to wander through the woods until a chance encounter with a forestry worker, who brought them back to the reserve.

I never dared ask Laurie what her feelings were both during those four days of action stations and after Laura and Nicole's return. How was she able to surmount the awful feeling of déjà-vu, the horror of seeing a pattern repeat itself; pain reawakened, the onslaught of memories; then a bitterness that cannot be spoken? Pam had no qualms about speaking up; she told reserve chief Gilbert Whiteduck point blank how much she wished people had mobilized in the same way back then—even though, when all was said and done, the two young women were not found by the search parties but by a chance encounter with a forestry worker. Had Laurie and Bryan known that same support and assistance, whatever the outcome, they would have been better able to weather the storm and feel part of a community, a society.

In response to the feelings of abandonment that have haunted Laurie and the immense frustration she has struggled to overcome year after year, reserve chief Gilbert and police chief Gordon have countered with a sincere "We tried our best at that period of time." Gilbert criss-crossed the countryside with Bryan on the lookout for the slightest trace; he organized the first press conference, was part of every ground search. "In my mind, I've replayed the investigation into Maisy and Shannon's disappearance a thousand times, thinking of the new strategies, the new approaches," Gordon explained. "It would be right away Montreal, Montreal comes down, right away shuts down the crime scene, does all this magical stuff for footprints, bloodstains . . ." Yet the SQ assured me that there are no more resources today than in 2008. Simply put, the Maniwaki and Kitigan Zibi police forces did not realize the urgency of the situation and did not pull the proper strings or call on the appropriate teams.

With the coming of night, and snow still falling outside the police station on this January 24, Gordon suddenly said, "I knew Maisy. I coached her for summer baseball."

"What was she like?"

"She was very active, personable." He smiled. "Really, really into joking stuff, she was really, really bubbly, happy-go-lucky, she was having fun, she never really had issues with her friends, she was very outgoing. She was not a quiet child, that's for sure! She was very fun," he laughed. "I enjoyed seeing her every time she came to play baseball. She could be mischievous . . . you had to keep your eye on her. She reminded me of my granddaughter. I knew she was having problems with her mom, but she was a nice girl, and I was surprised at what happened." He caught himself, "She *is* a nice girl. For now, we can still talk about her in the present."

*
*　*
*

In the fall of 2008, Maniwaki's police likely didn't push their investigation because they didn't see enough reason for concern in the disappearance of two Indigenous girls. Too far removed. Gordon and his team took too long to grasp the gravity of the situation for nearly opposite reasons: because Gordon knew Maisy well, he couldn't imagine that anything serious might have happened to the young girl—a teen going through a crisis, yes, but happy-go-lucky, active. Too close.

9
TORONTO
December 18, 2013

"Isn't he handsome?" Laurie says with a laugh. She looks fondly at the picture of the young journalist with brown hair and blue eyes, Brendan Kennedy, who covered Maisy and Shannon's disappearance for the *Ottawa Citizen*. Ten articles in eleven months. If Laurie's voice betrays some emotion, it's because Kennedy, a young intern at the time, did the exact opposite of what most other journalists used to do when an Indigenous woman went missing or was murdered: he persevered and followed the file with sensitivity. But he left Ottawa after his tenth article, the most important one, written for the anniversary of the girls' disappearance. He now works in Toronto for the *Toronto Star*, where he's responsible for reporting on the Queen City's baseball team, the Blue Jays.

However, even Kennedy's invaluable contributions could not compete with the media deluge that accompanied the murder or flight of non-Indigenous youth, especially when they are white. In her open letter, Laurie refers to the level of police mobilization when video-game addict Brandon Crisp ran away from home, or when two young white women, Ardeth Wood and Jennifer Teague, were murdered in Ottawa in 2003 and 2005; had Laurie read the Francophone press, she would probably have been struck by the massive SQ deployment in 2009 in the search for young David Fortin, whose face appeared next to Maisy's on posters put up in airports by Quebec's missing children organization, Enfant-Retour Québec.

Since police and media often feed off each other where missing person cases are concerned, the names and pictures of the same four young white people also flooded newspapers and TV screens for months afterwards.

And then there's Boomer, the lion cub.

December 18, 2013, at 2:59 p.m.
Hi Emmanuelle,

Sorry for the delay in getting back to you. I'm happy with my comments being on the record. . . .

I covered the second press conference on the one-month anniversary. From there I continued covering Maisy and Shannon's story. I actually hadn't heard about their disappearance before that second press conference. . . .

My answer to your second question will be a bit mixed. I agree with Laurie to some extent, but not fully. The cases are difficult to compare because of some key differences . . . . [Brandon

*Crisp's] case generated far more media coverage
than Maisy and Shannon, and I think it's fair
to say that was due, at least in part, to inherent
racism. But there were other differences, mainly
in how the local police agencies responded to the
missing person report and how that affected media
coverage. First of all, Brandon's parents reported
him missing the morning after he left the house.
In Maisy and Shannon's case, they had already
been gone for a few days before police were called.
Police also began to search for Brandon immediately, alerting the media in the process. The initial
response from both the Kitigan Zibi police and
the Sûreté du Québec (the provincial police) was
that Maisy and Shannon had probably run away
and would likely return. That itself speaks to
racist ideas about young Aboriginal women, even
among the reserve police. But the fact that neither
police agency investigating the matter showed
any urgency in finding Maisy and Shannon or
engaging the media certainly played a role in the
coverage. Brandon's story also included the sal-
acious element of video-game addiction, which
was, unfortunately, more of a hot-button topic
than the entrenched poverty and alienation of
Aboriginal youth and the crisis of murdered and
missing Aboriginal women. . . .*

*I tried as best I could to tell Maisy's and
Shannon's stories with compassion. I wanted to
portray them and their families accurately, but*

also with respect. It was also important for me to point out how inept and apathetic the two police agencies were in their investigation, which was further complicated by messy jurisdictional issues.

With all due respect to Laurie, I disagree with her about Boomer the Lion. I see her point, for sure, but considering how rare it is for a lion to be on the loose in Ottawa, of course it was going to be covered by all local media. But there's no reason why they couldn't also provide regular updates on Maisy and Shannon. . . .

I had to fight to get monthly updates in the paper and I wrote and reported my final feature on the one-year anniversary of their disappearance entirely on my own time. I worked two weeks of night shifts so I could travel to Kitigan Zibi during the day and return back to Ottawa to work my night shift. There was almost zero interest from my editors in this story. Whether that was due to latent racism or my editors simply not valuing a story that had little in the way of news, I'm not sure. I left the Ottawa Citizen *to take a job at the* Toronto Star *soon after finishing my last feature on Maisy and Shannon and never discussed with my editors why they had such little interest in the story . . .*

Hopefully this is helpful . . .

Brendan Kennedy

The "almost zero interest" referred to by Kennedy is all the more remarkable considering that his then newspaper, the *Ottawa Citizen,* had filled pages and pages a few years earlier with the stories of Ardeth Wood and Jennifer Teague. Researcher Kristen Gilchrist compared their media coverage to that given three young Indigenous women murdered in Saskatchewan: Daleen Bosse, Melanie Geddes and Amber Redman.[1] The six women (Alicia Ross was the third white woman in the sample, murdered in 2005) were either working or enrolled in school, and were neither runaways nor sex workers. Over a set period of time, the three white women's names were mentioned six times more than those of the three Indigenous women. The three white women had 187 articles devoted to them in the local press, while 53 articles were written about the three young Indigenous women. The young white woman who received the least media coverage was the subject of 33 articles, while the young Indigenous woman with the most coverage was the subject of 26 articles. All other indicators follow the same pattern: the headlines, poignant where the young white women were concerned ("Jenny we love you, we miss you"), factual for the young Indigenous women ("RCMP identifies woman's remains"); effusive adjectives for the white women (Alicia is "a lily among the thorns" with a "luminous smile") and conventional for the Indigenous women ("shy, nice, caring, a good mom, pretty, educated and positive"). Oversized pictures for the first group, passport size for the others. The placement of articles: between reports on a snowstorm and vintage cars for the young Indigenous girls; on the front page or those immediately following for the young white girls. And so it goes. By way of the only "consolation prize," Kristen Gilchrist observes that in twelve of the articles on the deaths of Daleen, Melanie and Amber, journalists readily mentioned the structural violence faced by Indigenous women.

News coverage in 2014—reports from the special committee and the RCMP, the report from the UN's Special Rapporteur on Human Rights for Indigenous Peoples, the fallout from the murder of young Tina Fontaine, the incredible story of Rinelle Harper surviving a brutal attack—saw an increase in the number of articles dealing with the issue of murdered and missing Indigenous women, often illustrated with Maisy and Shannon's faces. Their youth, the fact they had disappeared at the same time, the picture of an emotional Laurie brandishing "Missing" posters on the steps to Parliament, all explain their iconic presence. However, other than in the compassionate yet true-to-life portraits drawn by Kennedy, the public never learned much about the girls.

We find ourselves in a situation contrary to the one described in the French *"mort kilométrique"* theory, whereby a tragedy that occurs just around the corner is said to have much more impact than a death on the other side of the planet; the media are well aware of the principle, obsessed as they are with "staying close to the reader." Yet in the case of murdered Indigenous women, the theory no longer applies, or rather the distance separating Indigenous families (even in the heart of urban settings) from white readers counts three, four, five times more. The Indigenous world is foreign to Canadians, likely even more so than that of immigrants from Asia or Africa; resentment is strong towards First Nations, reproached for not abiding by the social pact while depending on federal subsidies they are accused of wasting; there is little comprehension that their communities are sometimes no better than Third-World villages located a few short kilometres from highly prosperous oil reserves; their fates are often marked by misfortune, even where financial resources exist, as with the James Bay Cree; their members are overrepresented in the prison system. So the silence is fuelled by the difficulty of identifying with Indigenous communities, a bitter stupefaction in the face of the cultural chasm that still exists after over four hundred years of cohabitation, and ignorance around dispossession and the trauma caused by residential schools.

January 30, 2014, 2:03 p.m.
Hi Emmanuelle,

I'm extremely sorry I didn't answer these questions last month. . . .

I decided to work on Maisy and Shannon's story on my own time because I felt it was an important story that needed to be told as comprehensively as possible. I would have preferred to do it as part of my paid duties at the Ottawa Citizen, *but when I realized that wasn't possible I didn't feel I had much of a choice. I didn't want the story to go untold and I felt it deserved more than just a passing, intermittent attention.*

Regarding the interest of my editors, I should clarify a few things: My editors did assign me to the second press conference (I believe it was held in early October, a month after they went missing; it was the first story I wrote on Maisy and Shannon), and when I pitched updates, they usually allowed me to write those stories as part of my regular shift. Where they would not grant me paid time to work on the stories was for the in-depth feature I wrote on the anniversary of their disappearance. . . . I should also point out that the paper was interested enough in the story to publish my feature on a full two-page spread. The assignment editors did not offer a specific reason for denying my request to work on the feature during my regular shift, but my understanding was that it was because I was still an intern at the paper and my role was primarily to cover daily news. . . .

I hope that helps. Let me know if you have any other questions.

BK

Ultimately, local newspapers have a tough time investing in complex stories and making them both moving and easy-to-read. Vulnerable young women, whether Indigenous or otherwise, come with complex baggage. To tell the story of the murders of blonde Ardeth and Jennifer, one a PhD student in philosophy, the other a soccer champion, is to broach the unthinkable, something that should never have happened; they didn't live in one of those underprivileged neighbourhoods where men kill women to assuage their rage against society; these virginal young women simply encountered an evil man at the worst possible moment. Telling Shannon and Maisy's story called for other ingredients. The reserve and its damaged, frustrated young men; the Algonquin community's proximity to a small white town; Shannon's broken parents; the unchecked emancipation of a precociously independent Maisy, as is often the case with young Indigenous girls; the trauma caused by colonial history and handed down from one generation to the next. Was there a genuine desire to enter into the story in all its complexity and make readers work? Was there a will to transport readers elsewhere? When articles on the murders of young Indigenous women rely on such psychosocial ingredients and invoke "at-risk behaviour," they forget to describe what the girls had in common with an Ardeth or a Jennifer: their tastes, their likes, their talents. Maisy and Shannon drank, smoked marijuana and hung out with bad boys, yet Maisy played the clarinet, Shannon rode horses; Maisy dreamed of becoming a fashion designer, Shannon belonged to the cadets; Maisy could sew complex, elaborate outfits, Shannon was going into nursing; Maisy loved to draw. Often the families of murdered or missing Indigenous girls mention the lack of curiosity shown by journalists, who generally confine their efforts to reporting on the scars. Conversely, other families distrust the media and are little inclined to fuel such storytelling.

Two editorials reflect a certain exasperation and convey the cultural and social chasm. In the space of a few months in 1992, three young Indigenous women, sex workers, were raped and brutally murdered in Saskatoon by serial killer John Crawford (Shelley Napope, Eva Taysup, Calinda Waterhen). During both the investigation and the trial, media coverage was extremely sparse, especially when compared to the coverage of trials of Canadian serial killers who murdered white women (the Paul Bernardo trial, for example). When criticism reached the ears of *Star Phoenix* editorial writer Les MacPherson, he justified the silence by blaming "the nearly total absence of connections between the victims [Aboriginal] and the mainstream community." These women, he said, "inhabited an isolated underworld where people routinely dropped out of sight. [They] did not maintain close contact with their immediate families. They were not expected home for dinner. Rather than condemning white folks for not much caring about murdered Indian women," he asks, "Who cared for them when they were still alive?"[2]

"They were not expected home for dinner" and so did not deserve media attention. MacPherson manages both to let his societal racism show and to miss the target, incapable as he is of imagining that bonds can be maintained between young sex workers and their parents (and yet that was the case for Crawford's victims). In an unsigned editorial in the *Ottawa Citizen*—not authored by Brendan Kennedy—a much less outrageous yet similar take can be found, this time explaining the lower level of police involvement in Shannon and Maisy's case. The bias is favourable: the editorialist writes that "Native people are right to think that if a pair of middle-class white girls vanished from some urban neighbourhood, you wouldn't see any police complacency."[3] However, hoping to strike a balance, leery of being too politically correct or obliging, the author then points at what led the girls to adopt risky behaviour: parental neglect, failings and trauma—Maisy's dropping out, Bryan's alcoholism, etc. "Even the most responsive police departments, enlightened government agencies and well-meaning social workers are not always able to write a happy ending." Before the above conclusion, he wrote, "As for Maisy . . . she seemed to have no place to call home. She left the reserve to move in with a boyfriend, then abandoned that situation after one month to try living with her grandmother." Maisy, the editorial suggests, was not expected home for dinner either.

Yet Maisy, the "outta control" teenager, as her father, Rick, wrote in one message, was in no way abandoned. Laurie's greatest hope was for her eldest to return home, and she had contacted social services to that end. Maisy spent most of the summer of 2007 with Rick in Ontario; he, too, hoped she would move back in with him; the young girl had been cared for for months at Lisa's house—and the dinners prepared by Lisa, grandmother and cook, were well worth coming home to. In both cases, it was the view that no family bonds could survive amidst chaos—or, at the very least, that the chaos justified the journalists and police officers giving up.

It is easier to give up on Indigenous peoples than on oneself (for one's ignorance and inadequacies).

Having spent time in the community, Brendan Kennedy played from another songsheet: by listening to Laurie's pain and describing the young girls as complex individuals, he shifted the centre of gravity.[*]

January 30, 2014, 4:22 p.m.
Hi Emmanuelle,

I'm 29 now, almost 30. I was 24 when I first started reporting on Maisy and Shannon and 25 by the time I finished.

I don't know if it was the most emotional story I've ever covered, but it's definitely the story I most personally invested in. I would also

---

* Since the summer of 2014, as with other large newspapers in the country such as the *Globe and Mail* and the *Toronto Star*, the *Ottawa Citizen* has devoted several in-depth articles and editorials to missing and murdered Indigenous women. Overall, we can assume that if two young Indigenous girls disappeared today under the same circumstances, media coverage would be much better than what we have seen in the past.

say it was one of the most unjust stories I've ever reported.

I don't remember reading any overtly racist stories in the media about Maisy and Shannon. I felt the discrimination more in the lack of attention and public apathy towards their disappearance.

I hope this helps you.

Good luck,

BK

10
Ottawa
January 31, 2014

Maria Jacko, Maisy's aunt, was already living in Ottawa when her beloved niece disappeared. The 140 kilometres separating her from Kitigan Zibi added to her feelings of helplessness.

Propelled by phenomenal energy—was it the energy of despair or of the accomplished athlete she is, or the energy of resilience? (Maria had overcome much, having lost her mother when she was seven and a partner shortly before her niece's disappearance, and having grown up in a foster home)—Maria threw herself into the search as if it were one of the marathons she runs, even though this particular race had no end in sight. Initially, she created the website findmaisyandshannon. com to gather leads and donations, then contacted various associations, including Ottawa's Search and Rescue Global 1 (SG1), an agency made up of volunteer search-and-rescue professionals.

Maria told me SG1 was surprised to hear from her. "They said that usually the police calls . . . The police get in touch with them to organize a search. So I told them about the situation, that the police and family weren't really working together at the time, you know . . . They asked if they could talk with the chief, so I set up a meeting with Chief Whiteduck and the Kitigan Zibi police. So we all had a meeting. There was me and my sister Penny, Laurie and Bryan. But it's so unfortunate it had to be that late. The first big ground search was in December 2008 in knee-deep snow."

It was also at Maria's urging that the RCMP added Maisy and Shannon's pictures to its website devoted to missing children. "They were surprised the police forces in Maniwaki and Kitigan Zibi hadn't contacted them," Maria added.

When I met her for the first time one winter morning, Maria was living with her three daughters in a small brick house in Ottawa. I waited for her at the door; she arrived in a yellow Jeep, wearing a fluorescent jacket, slim and gorgeous, and with her brown bangs looking more like twenty-five than thirty-eight. She had the look of a superhero straight out of the comics or a video game, and her face reminded me of her niece Maisy's. At the time, she was working as a lab technician while finishing her Master's degree at the University of Ottawa on success strategies employed by Indigenous athletes; a few months later, she was hired by the federal Aboriginal Affairs department. We sat down in her living room surrounded by native crafts and her high-strung poodles. Despite being in the eye of the hurricane, she spoke in a tone free from emotion, as though to temper her story.

Maria's house is only a few minutes away from Vanier, where Shannon's mother lives, a former bastion of the Francophone working class and a disadvantaged inner-city district inhabited by African and Asian immigrants and a number of Indigenous people. Since both families believed the girls might have travelled there, two searches had been organized, one by Laurie and the reserve police two weeks after the girls' disappearance, and another a month later by a local association. On Montreal Road, Vanier's main street (small kiosks and pizzerias, dollar stores, social housing, a concrete church), the groups put up posters and questioned shopkeepers and passersby. Thanks to the website, the newspaper articles and the posters, people from all over who thought they had seen the girls contacted Maria for months afterward.

Maria kept hopping into her car at each sighting. Police ineptitude turned her into the family detective. A call came in about a young girl wearing a hoodie loitering in the street; yes, she looked like Shannon, but it wasn't her. The barmaid at the Star Palace, a karaoke club on Montreal Road where Indigenous youth hung out, told her a girl with a scar had seen Shannon and Maisy in a crackhouse, and Maria hung around the Star Palace for weeks, hoping to bump into the girl with the scar, to no avail. Imaginations worked overtime in Vanier. An Inuit woman from the neighbourhood claimed she had spent several days with Maisy and Shannon, who, she said, had stolen $12,000 from a Kitigan Zibi smoke shop and were walking around with disposable cellphones. When questioned by police, she confessed she'd made it all up.

Then there was the employee from a Hull movie theatre on the Quebec side of the river who called Maria, saying he'd just seen the girls walk in with a group, she had to come right away. Maria drove half an hour only to find a Maisy look-alike, shorter and chubbier.

"The most emotional time was when the SQ called Laurie about eight months after the disappearance to tell her Maisy might be in the Hull hospital," Maria continued in the same calm tone. "Laurie calls me from the reserve and I jump into my car right away. I was crying, my heart was beating fast. When I park, I'm thinking I'm about to see Maisie. I'm thinking 'Freak, this is true,' because I already had in my mind that they were gone . . . So I go there, and one of the cops says, 'She's not talking to us,' but I see a young girl lying in bed and it isn't Maisy, I can't remember the details, I don't know why she was there. Was she wearing handcuffs? No, I don't think so; I just asked her what her name was. She wouldn't talk to the police, but she answered me right away. Kayra, or something like that."

She remembered that "Kayra" came from Chisasibi, a Cree[1] reserve on Hudson Bay in northern Quebec, 1,270 km from Hull, twenty hours by car, six hours by plane, including stopovers. Why was she lying in a hospital bed? And all the girls mentioned by Maria—the girl with the scar, Kayra, who came from so far away, the Inuit trickster—were they ghosts tasked with leaving clues to be considered before starting up again, carrying on, looking elsewhere?

Maria added, "I talked to Eileen, a psychic, several times on the phone; she told me Shannon and Maisy were gone and were buried, not just under branches and stuff, but by a church. I went to see M., a well-known psychic from Ottawa who's been on the radio. M. told me they could still be alive and if they're dead, they could be buried in cement, he feels something about up north. I called a New York psychic that a missing children society put me in contact with. He said he didn't have any vibrations. I talked to maybe five different psychics, and every time I had to pay $100 or $150."

"Does Laurie know you consulted psychics?"

"Yes, but she doesn't believe in them. I never believed before either. Today, I don't know, I think they might help us. We talked to an Ojibwe medicine man, too. With him, we might do the shaking tent. He's seen things before. In Kitigan Zibi, some people have had visions, like my Aunt Ethel; she *saw* the girls' bodies on the tracks by Bryan and Shannon's apartment in Maniwaki. So we took a group of people, we had four-wheelers and shovels and everything. It was in the wintertime. We spent two days digging, we checked exactly where she looked and it wasn't . . . we didn't find anything. Ethel still believes that the bodies were there at one point."

Weekend after weekend, Maria had gone digging—literally—in Kitigan Zibi. She and her partner at the time participated with Bryan and other friends in fifty-odd search parties. She didn't dig just anywhere. She dug on land belonging to a Maniwaki hockey coach who committed suicide in prison after being convicted of raping a young girl; he was a suspect for a while, then cleared posthumously. For Maria, who had seen an anonymous letter describing in detail his behaviour the day after the disappearance, he was still a legitimate suspect. She didn't dig randomly. She'd bought a metal detector.

"We walked for miles down that road by the coach's land, didn't we, Maria?"

Maria and I were at Bryan's late that winter. He smiled at her. "Remember the time we got lost?"

She laughed.

"We should go back," said Bryan.

"I got a new lead. I found out he had a house in Egan-South" (a village adjacent to Maniwaki). "A new place to look. But you know, I left my metal detector in Ottawa."

"About the metal detector . . . there's a downside. The only metal Shannon had on her when she went missing was her necklace. I think it had a silver chain, I bought it for her at a pow wow, and it had a grain of rice I had her name engraved on. But the detector should be able to detect that, right? It works. Last time, remember . . ."

"We found something, it was beeping, we looked at each other, so happy . . . but it was just a bit of fencing."

They both laughed.

11
SIX NATIONS
March 14, 2014

It took me months to find the words to write to Rick Jacko, Maisy's father, Laurie's first husband. He left the reserve when Maisy and Damon were still little. He was said to be fragile, devastated by his daughter's disappearance. But almost as soon as I sent him my request, his answers came rolling in, short successive messages at intervals of several hours or weeks.

He wrote to me from Six Nations, the Mohawk community in Ontario where he lives now.

> *Question #1. In the summer of 2007, I went to pick her up from Kitigan Zibi. She stayed with us for a few months. Summertime, I make a living selling my crafts, cards, decals, stickers. I took her everywhere with me, she loved that! I wanted to show her what was going on in my life. You know, I never talk to people like I'm talking*

to you. It makes me cry . . . All my friends always ask me about this and I change the subject. It's something that is really too hard to deal with. The last time I saw Maisy . . . was on my fridge. She gave me a picture of when she was a baby, me holding her . . . Best gift ever! The picture's still here. I will continue to give you information about my first-born as I can. All at once is kinda hard. You already have me tearing up.

Rick inserted the picture in the body of the message. A tiny, serious Maisy, her small head resting in her father's hand.

Question #2. The last time I saw her . . . That summer she came here . . . I remember how she had turned into such a beautiful girl, and how many lil punk kids I'd have to fight off, her getting mad at me . . . I remember her trying to pull tricks on me, like I didn't know them all anyway. We walked and talked, played football, she is an excellent runner!!! I'd let her drive my truck, she said she was happy with me but being so far away from home made her sad . . . She decided to go back to Kitigan Zibi. I just wish she would have met Wiley, her new little sister and her brother Manny. I know she would love them!!!!!

Question #3. I live seven hours away from Kitigan Zibi. That there hurts. I don't like putting

my face on TV. But yes, I did the searches, the
vigils, the walks and runs . . . Every day I cry for
that girl. I miss her so much!!!! I may continue
beyond this, lose a child and see how much you
can live a regular life!!! I remember as a baby,
she was just a loveable baby, so quiet, always
smiling, always loved, giving hugs n kisses . . .

Rick made small crafts—like little purple feathers to
wear on jackets—bearing Shannon's and Maisy's names,
which he sold at auctions held to raise money for the
families of missing and murdered women.

The next message, months later:

Remember you had asked me where I was when
I found out when Maisy went missing?? I had
got into trouble and I was in jail in Toronto. I
had to wait till November 24 to get out, and I
made my way up there to Kitigan Zibi as soon
as I got out. Worst months of my life.

Jailed on a drunk-driving charge, Rick was out in
time to take part in the extensive ground searches held
in December and May in Kitigan Zibi. He was there,
too, anonymous and silent, walking through the forest
and digging through the undergrowth. Montreal activist Maya Rolbin-Ghanie wrote: "Towards the end of the
search that day while we were sitting around taking a
break, a man that several of us admitted later to wanting
to talk to, revealed his identity. Before that, he had been

keeping to himself, and seemed to want it that way. But when I finally asked where he was from, he told us that he was Maisy's dad. He lives in Six Nations now, but had come for the search. He looked very young, and he also looked very tired."[1]

12

In the Woods, Kitigan Zibi
May 2, 2009

I have in front of me pictures from the May 2009 ground search through the Kitigan Zibi forest. The intent gaze of jacket-clad walkers listening to their instructions, each one carrying a big stick; then the same people bent over the ground as they searched through thick woods of tall thin trunks. There were 240 in all, residents from the reserve and Maniwaki as well as volunteers from Ottawa and Montreal.

Among them, by Laurie, Rick and Maria's side, was Maryanne Pearce. She had already begun work on her doctoral thesis into Canada's missing and murdered women.[1] A civil servant with the federal government who specialized in issues around health and violence against women, Pearce designed health and economic development programs for Indigenous communities. Over seven years, she had built a database of missing and murdered women for her thesis; in doing so, she discovered that approximately a quarter of the women were Indigenous. I told myself that, by participating in the ground search, Maryanne had jumped into the fray; her statistics and the exhausting gathering of grim data were taking a more tangible turn.

A wooded area where ground searches were conducted.

"There are many stories whose faces and names haunt me. But when it involves youth, they have the whole world in front of them ... and Maisy and Shannon are very similar to the age of my daughter so ... the story about those girls had something that really touched me, just a little bit deeper. And there was something concrete I could do."

We were in a small pizzeria in Ottawa on January 31, 2014. Pearce, in her forties, blonde with a beautiful face that showed her years, spoke quickly, intensely. "Everybody met at 7:30 in the morning. Amnesty International had chartered three buses, people from SAR Global 1 told people what to wear, what to bring: a big stick or a broom handle. In the bus were activists from NWAC, Amnesty . . . All in all, we were people more used to sitting behind a desk. There was a woman sitting next to me on the bus . . . she was there because her cousin had been murdered somewhere in Labrador. She had waited for the unknown . . . until her remains were found. She was just a nice woman who wanted to help. When we got there after a two-hour trip, Laurie stepped onto each bus. She spoke to us in a very . . . you could feel her strength, her energy. She spoke very well. She thanked us, even knowing what we were looking for in the woods, the remains of her daughter and her daughter's friend . . . In the bus, after she had gone, it was very, very quiet, and many of us had lumps in our throat and tears in our eyes . . ."

"So you walked and walked . . ."

"Yes. I had never done one before. My health . . . I got sick a couple of years ago. I don't think I'll be able to do it again. We were in the woods very close to the community centre on the reserve. We were basically arm's-length apart so we started, we touched fingers and we walked slowly. You might have to slow down because there were times where there'd be a ravine . . .

I think there were ten of us per squad in a line, looking and digging with our sticks. We went through water, a lot of water and stuff like that . . . The people from SAR Global 1 had GPS units so they could identify the areas that had been searched. They had radios to be able to contact each other."

"Did anyone find things or see things?"

"Pieces of clothing, shoes, garbage . . . Nothing significant."

"Do you remember how you felt?"

"I think everybody wanted . . . I think everybody felt that they wanted to find something that would help provide an answer . . . but nobody wanted something to be found that would show that they were no longer here. For me, it was very, very emotional."

Meeting Maryanne, I felt like the two of us belonged to the same club: so I wasn't the only one who knew the names and stories of the dead women and girls by heart and who dreamed of them at night; in that regard, Maryanne was years ahead of me. As we picked at our salads, too absorbed in our discussion to eat, I interviewed her on her just-published thesis, which was already making waves—this was before the RCMP report—because it revealed the highest percentage ever reported of Indigenous women among missing and murdered women. "When I speak about my thesis," she told me, "I'm not speaking as a federal public servant or as a spokesperson for the government. You see, I keep my work as a public servant and my thesis work separate."

It was more complicated than that, however, something I only discovered reading the first pages of her thesis; I was taken aback at the many intimate and personal details she revealed, not during our informal discussion in a restaurant, but in the very body of her academic work. In the first chapter, she mentions her job as a volunteer accountant and treasurer for Ottawa's Indigenous women's shelters and adds:

> I have long been concerned with issues of poverty, violence and the mental and physical health of women, with a particular emphasis on the most vulnerable: women who are homeless, addicted, suffering mental health issues, fleeing violence, involved in survival sex work or of Aboriginal ethnicity . . . . Like the women about whom I discuss within this dissertation, I experienced considerable physical and sexual violence in my youth, barely escaping death on several occasions. At 18, I dropped out of high school and moved to B.C., where I worked multiple jobs, hitchhiked daily as the only mode of transport in Whistler, lived in my car and had a child at age 20. I have engaged in sex work, struggled with addictions, mental health issues or been part of the child welfare system. Thankfully, I had strong ties and support from family and friends who assisted me in leaving an abusive relationship. At 22, I began university as a single mother of an 18-month-old child.

Searches were also conducted near Lake Pitobig. Maisy lived by the lakeshore with her grandmother.

And Maryanne Pearce's second life began: studies, marriage, a second child. "My personal history is not intended to be a confessional," she continues, "but having trained first as an anthropologist, I know it is important for a researcher to provide an audience with one's personal starting point. The women who have been murdered, gone missing or are at risk of experiencing violence are not merely subjects of research but truly are my Sisters in Spirit." Here, she is referring to the name of the NWAC program. A footnote on page 3 of her thesis sheds light on the book as a whole. She explains that her mother, grandmother and aunts all fostered children. Then, "As an aboriginal family, social workers preferred to place Aboriginal children with us if possible; I personally had 12 foster siblings before age five."[2]

"Yes, I'm Aboriginal on my mother's side," Maryanne confirmed. "On the other side, my ancestry is Celtic."

So Maryanne with her blond curls has, in fact, Mohawk blood; she is not just an engaged and resolute public servant; she knows inside and out how fragility and the paths to vulnerability accumulate, something I was only discovering. I had been wrong; by joining the ground search party, she was not "jumping into the fray" and leaving her databases behind for a dose of reality. She was continuing on a quest for redress. Aware from a very young age of the fragility found in the Indigenous world, a victim of sexual abuse herself, Maryanne now devoted her life's work to abused, lost, murdered and missing women.

At the pizzeria, she added, "I look after dogs, too, strays."

13
YORK FACTORY, HUDSON BAY
February 5, 1717

Amber grew up in northern Alberta on the shores of Lake Athabaska; it is said that Thanadelthur came from the shores of the same lake, but it is more likely that she was born in northern Manitoba. Both women belonged to the Dene people of northwestern Canada. They both died at around age twenty; one murdered, the other felled by disease.

Any resemblance between the two ends there. Amber's bones were found by chance two years after her disappearance south of Edmonton. Thanadelthur's bones, duly honoured, piously buried, lie next to Hudson Bay. Times were different then. While Thanadelthur perished in 1717, Amber died in 2010. Between the two dates, the winds of conquest transformed North America and destroyed the status of Indigenous women.

In November 1714, at the age of eighteen or nineteen, Thanadelthur escaped from the Cree village that had captured and enslaved her, and found refuge in a Hudson's Bay Company fur-trading post at York Factory. To facilitate trade, the company hoped to broker a peace deal between the Cree and Chipewyan peoples. Thanadelthur's assistance was invaluable: she knew the peoples and the territory; she spoke Chipewyan (her own language), English and Cree. She eventually headed up an eleven-month peace expedition plagued by starvation, disease and deadly conflicts between the two nations. It is said that she faced every challenge head on and galvanized her troops. Thanadelthur died of illness on February 5, 1717, as she prepared for another expedition, and her death shook James Knight, chief factor of the fur-trading post. "I am almost ready to break my heart. . . . She was one of a Very high Spirit and of the Firmest Resolution that ever I see Any Body in my Days and of great Courage & forecast, also endowed with an Extraordinary Vivacity of Apprehension, Readily takeing anything right as was proposed to her & Presently Give her Opinion whether it would doo or not."[1] Her death, Knight added, was a great loss for the company.

The celebration of Thanadelthur, another "facilitator of colonization," along with American heroines Pocahontas and Sacagawea, can be seen as an irritant by some. These are women who saved settlers' lives, negotiated commercial trade, opened the way to the development of resources that until then had belonged to First Peoples. However, her story shows the power held by Indigenous women at the time and the high regard accorded them both by their communities and by the colonizers. Far more than keepers of hearth and home, they played a leading role in the fur trade, a role only discovered and spelled out much later by Canadian historians.[2] Beginning in the sixteenth century, the French and English *coureurs des bois*, who bought beaver pelts from the Indigenous peoples, owed their economic activity and their very survival in the forest to the First Nations women they teamed up with. These women hunted ("My woman brought home 8 hares and 14 partridges," boasted an English merchant in 1815),[3] harvested wild rice in marshes; made nets, fished and dried the catch; prepared pemmican, the famous mixture of dried bison meat and melted fat; knew how to tan, preserve and sew hides together; built canoes and navigated. "They pitch our tents, make and mend our clothing, keep us warm at night; and, in fact, there is no such thing as travelling any considerable distance, or for any length of time, in this country without their assistance," wrote a *coureur des bois* in 1770.[4] Some, like Thanadelthur, were such highly regarded interpreters and diplomats that competing fur-trading posts fought to work with them.

*

* *

*

Amber Alyssa Tuccaro, born into the Lake Athabasca community of Fort Chipewyan[5] in northern Alberta, disappeared in August 2010 at the age of twenty-one, 293 years after Thanadelthur's death.

In 2012, a group of horseback riders discovered her skeleton lying in a field. At the time of her disappearance, round-cheeked Amber lived with her baby in Fort McMurray, a town of eighty thousand to the south of her village and a Mecca for oil produced from the tar sands, the country's war chest (in fact, this is one last thing she had in common with Thanadelthur: both lived alongside white people busy exploiting the country's natural resources).

While the young eighteenth-century Indigenous woman led more than 150 men under extreme conditions and brought about the reconciliation of reluctant warriors, Amber most likely perished as a result of male violence. In 2012, the RCMP made public the recording of a phone conversation that took place the night of her disappearance on August 18, 2010. Although the source of the recording is not specified, the understanding is that it must have come from one of Amber's friends who received her distress call. At the time, Amber was in a car with a stranger who must have picked her up hitchhiking not far from Edmonton, a six-hour drive from Fort McMurray, where she was spending a few days for medical reasons. She can be heard worrying about the route the driver has taken. "Yo, where are we going? You better not be taking me anywhere I don't wanna go! Then where the fuck are these roads going to? I wanna go into the city!" she cries as the car turns down a gravel road unlikely to lead to downtown Edmonton, where she planned to spend the evening.

The RCMP put up two billboards in the region, asking the public to listen to the recording and help identify the driver.[6] But the investigation was so inept, particularly in the months immediately following the disappearance, that Amber's mother eventually filed a complaint against the police in March 2014. By the winter of 2015, we still don't know who the young woman's killer was.

*
*   *
*

Some murdered or missing Indigenous women have French names from their *coureurs des bois* ancestors, those who not only married Indigenous women but espoused their culture and fathered Métis children; so from the seventeenth to the nineteenth century, the *coureurs des bois* and their female companions embodied the small forest- and lake-based society in which the settlers adopted the lifestyle of the colonized.

Glenda Morrisseau (Manitoba, 1991), Pauline Brazeau (Alberta, 1977), Rose Decoteau (Alberta, 2005), Alicia Courtoreille-Brignall (B.C., 2007), Marie Goudreau (Alberta, 1976), Myrna Letandre (Manitoba, 2006), Amber Guiboche (Manitoba, 2010), Fonassa Bruyère (Manitoba, 2007).

Did they know the meaning of their surnames?

Did they know of equality lost?

*
*   *
*

Be that as it may, that small protocolonial civilization soon began to exhibit worrying signs, as researcher Marie-France Labrecque describes: "As soon as the Europeans arrived, the men demanded access to Indigenous women to satisfy their sexual needs, forcing them to prostitute themselves."[7] Maryanne Pearce cites other research on the same issue: "The practice of Indians squatting with the families around trading posts and selling the services of their wives and daughters for pennies with which to buy booze is a well-documented fact."[8] And, "In 1886, traffic of Indian women became a national scandal which involved employees of the Indian Affairs Department."[9] So at the same time that the wives of the *coureurs des bois* were seen as indispensable partners, other young women were already being sexually exploited.

Until the conquest shattered Indigenous social structures, women were the mainsprings of their own communities. Not that I'm speaking of an Eden where gender equality reigned supreme. Roles were very different, but each gender's work was appreciated and a whole array of political and societal authority was assigned to women—Iroquois nations were clearly matriarchal, for example. Among certain peoples, women's relative freedom of choice in affairs of the heart surprised Europeans. As the conquest turned to tilling the land and drafting "Indian" legislation, women lost what was theirs (the possibility of owning land and transferring ownership to their daughters, leading religious ceremonies, organizing agricultural activity and village life, building dwellings, counselling chiefs during conflicts with other nations). They also lost the special esteem they had benefitted from in their communities for centuries in the spiritual realm largely because they were seen to be closer to nature, a central element in Indigenous culture. The white population interpreted their relative sexual freedom as debauchery. The fiction of the depraved "squaw" was born.

It is a fiction that can still be found today. Many advertising images represent women made up or dressed as Indigenous women, looking lascivious and sexually available. "The portrayal of the squaw is one of the most degraded, most despised and most dehumanized anywhere in the world. The 'squaw' is the female counterpart to the Indian male 'savage' and as such she has no human face; she is lustful, immoral, unfeeling and dirty. Such grotesque dehumanization has rendered all Native women and girls vulnerable to gross physical, psychological and sexual violence," writes Manitoba researcher Emma LaRocque.[10]

*
* *
*

For the space of three frozen winters on the shores of Hudson Bay, Thanadelthur embodied a certain equality between pioneers and colonized, between men and women. A distant memory. The 1876 Indian Act (born of the 1857 Act to Encourage the Gradual Civilization of the Indian Tribes) obliged "bands" to set up exclusively male governments and dismantle the skillful distribution of roles recognizing the importance of each and every man and woman. In so doing, it ruled that women who married white men or "non-status" Indians would lose their Indian status,[11] and therefore the right to live in their community or have access to services reserved for Indigenous communities; they would lose their cultural identity. Indigenous men who married non-Indians lost nothing. This unbelievable abomination lasted until 1985 and, according to Amnesty International, uprooted "tens of thousands of Indigenous women, jeopardizing their ties to their families and increasing their dependence on their spouses."[12] "Ottawa made the decision that women had to choose between their identity and their heart," as Aurélie Arnaud of Quebec Native Women (QNW) explained it to me. "Still today, unions between status and non-status Indians mean that the children and grandchildren of mixed couples lose their Indian status. It's a way for the government to reduce the number of status Indigenous people living on reserves and, one day, of taking our land," she states.[13]

In the space of a century, women were reduced to an underclass in their own communities. The European patriarchy had taken root among Indigenous peoples.

When I met Craig Benjamin in the Ottawa offices of Amnesty International, he told me: "Where the perpetrators are Aboriginal, it does not mean that there was not an element of racism in the violence . . . Aboriginal men, no less than non-Aboriginal men, grow up in a broader media culture that has perpetuated really terrible images of Aboriginal women. That's a key factor."

It took me months to understand the full scope of his words as I dug deeper and deeper with each macabre discovery, like an appalled archaeologist . . . or a war correspondent.

Some two-dozen Indigenous women were gathered in a small room in the big red hotel located next to Highway 15 in the northern suburbs of Montreal. Three of them wore blue vests as "health support workers." "If you find anything disturbing or need support, they are there for you," one of the two facilitators[1] pointed out. The workshop on sexual violence was part of QNW's Annual General Meeting. In the audience were social workers, female band council chiefs and female activists, mostly Francophone, with some Anglophones, from Innu,[2] Algonquin and Inuit communities. This time, they were talking not only about the people they help but about themselves. "What is your biggest fear?" the facilitators asked each participant.

"I deal with sexual violence in my community and my fear is that it might happen at home in my family."

"I'm afraid for my little boy."

"I was sexually abused and gang raped when I was young in residential school, and I'm afraid I'll never be able to love again. I'm scared for my granddaughters, too."

"I have a niece who's growing up in an environment with a lot of alcohol . . . I'm afraid for her."

"No one talks about a very taboo subject, no one shines a light on it; in my community, young people come to see me with accounts of incest and suicide."

"In my community, things aren't okay, but no one talks about it."

"If we don't end the taboo around talk of sexual abuse, we'll keep on being colonized!"

As the facilitators listed recurring tragedies (young pregnant girls not even knowing they'd been raped because they were so drunk when it happened and who feel guilty instead of victimized; women who don't denounce their abusive spouse out of loyalty to their in-laws or for fear of being forced off the reserve with nowhere to go—no room in shelters—or seeing their children taken away) and the participants shared traumatic experiences, their stories were interspersed with laughter and joking. Crude jokes, black humour. These women, whose profession puts them at ground zero of the sexual abuse that destroys many Indigenous communities, burst into gales of joyous laughter.

Shell-shocked by the stories, overwhelmed by the women's resilience, I took next to no notes.

None of them saw the need to call on the services of the health support workers in their blue vests.

In her book *Kuessipan*, young Innu writer Naomi Fontaine tells of rape and of sex under the distorting influence of alcohol. "The undressing happens at night. Top and bottom stripped bare. Red cheeks. Warm tears. Dreams granted by keeping mouths shut. Saying no to fear. Sand to lie down on. Filth. The others gone before. Intoxication, red eyes. Gaps in memory. At night nothing to see, other than what hands can touch."[3] In a study on sexual abuse in Quebec's Indigenous reserves, the majority of people surveyed estimated that 50 to 70 percent of their community members, mostly women, have been victims.[4] I discovered, horrified, what seemed the height of self-annihilation: young teen girls prostituted by their families . . . under their own roofs.

That same day in that same place, another workshop with a troubling title: "Trafficking of Aboriginal Women."

In Canada.

I knew this was one of the theories around the disappearance of Shannon and Maisy, whose striking beauty is mentioned in every interview and every conversation. But I didn't believe it. I wanted to think it was all hyperbole.

Widia Larivière, our gentle auburn-haired not-yet-thirty co-facilitator, part-Algonquin, part-Québécois, is responsible for the QNW youth file, but is also a well-known activist in the Idle No More movement. She explained that Indigenous women are overrepresented among victims of Canada's sex trade; 90 percent of all underage—and thus exploited—sex trade workers are Indigenous. Widia listed off recruitment sites: bars, airports, bus stations, large logging camps in northern Quebec. She kept saying, "I can't believe it, the things I've read about, even in our own communities . . . I can't believe it." This case-hardened activist seemed profoundly shaken, but shaken into action. She was busy launching a bilingual prevention campaign entitled "I'm a proud Aboriginal woman and I'm not for sale."

After the meeting, I dove into three research reports with titles that stunned me: *Sacred Lives: Canadian Aboriginal Children & Youth Speak Out About Sexual Exploitation,*[5] "Domestic Sex Trafficking of Aboriginal Girls in Canada: Issues and Implications,"[6] *Trafficking of Aboriginal Women and Girls in Canada.*[7] The trafficking described by researchers is unlike that involving girls from Eastern Europe or Asia. No theft of passport or illegal confinement, few moves from one city to another. The researchers explain that, seen from afar, the trade looks like "ordinary" street sex work and since, in the Canadian consciousness, Indigenous women have been associated with sex trade work for so long, the powers that be and journalists have not seen it as coercive.

Yet the coercion is real: it lies mainly in the fact that pimps often get the young girls hooked on crack or crystal meth, the poor man's cocaine, before forcing them out on the streets to make money to pay for hits, often provided by the pimps themselves. Although the researchers focused their work on large Prairie cities—Winnipeg, Edmonton, Regina—where the Indigenous teen sex trade orchestrated by street gangs is visible, they also mention Montreal's airport as a prime recruitment centre because of the young Inuit girls who land there, fleeing the poverty or violence of their communities in Quebec's Great North. "Traffickers often know someone in the community who informs them about the plans of the girls moving to the city," said one social worker who spoke to researcher Anupriya Sethi. "Upon their arrival at the airport, traffickers lure the girls under the pretext of providing a place to stay . . . they are young, naïve and vulnerable in a new and big city. They are unsuspecting of the motives of the traffickers, since they belong to communities that have a culture of welcoming strangers."[8]

But the link to the originating community seems to be much stronger than a simple phone call between it and Montreal. Where street gangs are Indigenous, they come and go between the reserve and the big city: "Many girls get swept up in the movement by being encouraged to come to the city for parties and becoming sexually exploited," notes Annette Sikka. Worse yet: "In Edmonton . . . gangs threaten to tell young girls' families about their activities as a prostitute if they don't keep on working and supplying the gang with money. Often, the gangs that misled the young girls have ties with the originating community: the threat is very real," she adds.[9]

One can and must distinguish between this forced sex trade, a form of sexual exploitation, and "sex work," which some Indigenous women have chosen on their own terms.

*
*   *
*

However, the chaotic path followed by the most vulnerable young Indigenous girls includes time in what might be seen as a refuge: the group home/*foyer de groupe* or, in Quebec only, the *centre jeunesse*. "Having gone through the youth protection system is probably the one characteristic that girls who enter prostitution have in common," Annette Sikka writes. And so begins a downward spiral, a diabolical sequence of events that can ensnare boys as well, but to a lesser extent: the victim of sexual abuse in a family or community is placed in a group home, but the supervision provided there leaves much to be desired, so the young people become chronic runaways; traffickers and pimps lie in wait. The very structure of the homes means that young girls are sometimes told by their so-called boyfriends, predators who prowl around the homes, to recruit future prostitutes from among their friends.[10] I don't know whether Tina Fontaine, fifteen, found lifeless in the Red River in Winnipeg on August 17, 2014, was a victim of sexual abuse as a child. But by that time she had not been in her mother's care for five years, and her father had been murdered three years earlier; for the month prior to her disappearance, she had been living in a Winnipeg group home, and she had been sexually exploited in the weeks leading up to her murder. So Tina's fate is an outright contradiction of Prime Minister Stephen Harper's claim that there is no sociological aspect to the issue.

The spiral that leads from neglect or domestic violence to sexual exploitation on the streets is confirmed by the young people themselves in the disturbing report *Sacred Lives,* an account of conversations with 150 Indigenous youth in twenty-two Canadian cities and towns.

> *My abusers were abused; their abusers were abused, down the line. We're all hurting in one way or another, and I think that's why the cycle continues and turns (Female youth, Vancouver).*

> *I grew up . . . in an abusive family. My mom gave up on me when I was thirteen, and I started fixing. I was constantly being moved from foster home to foster home, and I had nobody to talk to about anything . . . . The money part of it (the sex trade) was in my hands for maybe fifteen minutes. I'd get it and go straight to the dealers (Female youth, Saskatoon).*

> *My stepfather was abused as a child, and he didn't know himself how to be a parent. So he did his best, which was basically what his father*

did to him. I think that things like this can be
prevented . . . my situation . . . if the cycle of
abuse is broken (Female youth, Halifax).[11]

The two workshops, two of many, that Saturday in
November in the big red hotel by the highway could have
been merged into one. They are two pieces of the same
puzzle; two successive stations on the same way of the
cross.

15
DESERT RIVER, MANIWAKI
January 25, 2014

Back in Maniwaki, *Pakwaun* was in full swing. The winter festival with the Algonquin name included a hockey game on the ice of Desert River, a vintage snowmobile show, a trampoline and bouncy castles for the children, strongman competitions and a hot dog dinner. The snow came down thick and fast; red-cheeked young couples drove around on mini 4-wheelers; in the sea of white faces, a few Kitigan Zibi families stood out, come with their little ones and their strollers. I walked up to the hot dog stand, where a dozen white men in their forties and fifties bustled around, and I spoke to them about Maisy and Shannon. They all remembered; some had helped raise money for the families. Later others confirmed the genuine empathy shown by the people of Maniwaki when the girls went missing. As for relations between the town and the reserve, they were good, yes, why? asked the man grilling hot dogs. He lived on the edge of the reserve and got along just fine with his Indigenous neighbour.

The man's idyllic description elicited a half-smile from Gilbert Whiteduck, Kitigan Zibi's band council chief; he preferred to talk about the "invisible wall" separating Maniwaki from the reserve. Because the Algonquins were colonized in English and are, for the most part, unilingual, they are not seen as potential employees by businesses and services in the small town, which is largely Francophone. "Yet we spend almost all our money in Maniwaki, that's where we go out to eat or to buy a car," Gilbert observed. Twenty percent of the clientele for the J.O. Hubert store on the main street— offering clothing, shoes, toys, bicycles, dishes and hardware—is Indigenous, explained owner Paul Hubert.

Before the reserve had its own general store, its members shopped in Maniwaki at places like the Poirier grocery store and frequented bars like the central hotel's tavern, where whites didn't go, in an atmosphere "worthy of apartheid," recalls one inhabitant who grew up in Maniwaki in the '60s. And Georges Lafontaine, a former journalist who now works for the Algonquin[1] nation's tribal council, remembers the Maniwaki Inn's discotheque in the '70s and '80s, when one section by the washrooms was understood to be reserved for "Indians," a section regulars called the Swamp. Times have changed, but the hostility—or ignorance—remains. "Actually, I'd call it solitude more than hostility," muses Georges Lafontaine. "Two solitudes. I know Algonquins and whites who've crossed paths for years on the streets of Maniwaki and have never said hello. The gulf is even deeper now. At one point, *Pakwaun* was a time when the two communities met. There was a big Algonquin feast, a beauty pageant that young girls from the reserve took part in," he continues. "Algonquin culture is visible during the festival. But people from the reserve feel they were on display and have gradually quit taking part." From Maniwaki's teachers, I heard whispers that Gilbert's arrival as head of the reserve had further poisoned relations between Kitigan Zibi and Maniwaki. I was made to understand that his radical stances, in particular on the issue of land claims and Indigenous rights, led to him turning down interesting co-operative educational projects. Mention was made of a past that would not heal.

Main Street, Maniwaki, where Maisy and Shannon were seen before the dance at the *polyvalente*.

*
*   *
*

In the nineteenth century, when settlers arrived and took up residence where the Desert River and Gatineau River meet, it was to trade with the Algonquins who hunted beaver, and to benefit from their knowledge. Home to the Hudson's Bay Company, to its fur traders and to logging companies, the small town mushroomed and, under the horrified gaze of the Oblate fathers, turned into something out of a Western movie with its fighting and boozing. The Oblates managed to turn it into a municipality with bylaws and enforcers establishing law and order. In 1853, the same Oblates, in their dubious dual roles of evangelizers and protectors, brought about the creation of a reserve for the "River Desert band," the Algonquin people living there.[2]

What is a reserve? A prison or a refuge? A place to hide away, or to cultivate one's identity, where pride can be maintained? A place where unemployment has reached record levels, but where seasonal work can be found, as in Kitigan Zibi? A place where some families combine social success and community-mindedness and others survive on welfare? A place that is hard to leave because of the problems posed by social integration elsewhere?

What is a reserve?

"Luc-Antoine Pakinawatik, a community chief in the mid-nineteenth century, saw the impact of development and colonization and thought that we really needed our own land," Gilbert explains. "Many families didn't welcome the idea of a reserve, but before long they were being put in jail for hunting and trapping in places they'd lost the right to . . . Plus, game wasn't as plentiful anymore because of all the logging. All the best trees were being cut down. So gradually, the Algonquins in the region moved here for protection. For us, the reserve was where we could keep hunting and fishing. For the government, it was a way of better controlling us."

Entering the reserve from the north.

*
* *
*

Gilbert was, in fact, my second interview in French with someone from the Anglophone community after Lisa Odjick (Little Grandma). Lisa had learned French as a child, playing with her Québécois neighbours; Gilbert owed his command of the language to playing hockey for Maniwaki.

"I was the only Native person on the team. They called me a savage! My parents didn't have the money to buy me equipment; we were really poor, that was the norm on the reserve. My gloves were made out of bamboo and hay and were always falling apart; that made the referees laugh . . . At high school in Maniwaki, I was told, 'Your best bet is to follow in your father's footsteps.' He worked in logging. There was so little work for us in the region, even in Ottawa, that people from the reserve travelled to the States for jobs; like my father, who built pipelines, railway tracks . . . Back then, I told myself that nothing would stop me."

Gilbert wasn't talking about some long-ago past, but of the colonial Canada he experienced during his childhood in the '60s. Anger had pushed him this far: a teacher, then director of education for Kitigan Zibi, then elected and re-elected chief.

"I remember we'd go to the Indian agent with my parents to get certain rights."

Indian agents were responsible for administering reserves for the government, and played the role of judge, coroner and police. Among others.

"He put his desk up on a dais and any Algonquin who went to see him had to talk up to him." (Gilbert pantomimed the situation, looking up at the ceiling.) "We were really afraid of him, he had so much power, so many contacts with business people, with the RCMP . . . No one dared cross him. Believe it or not, we had an Indian agent right up to 1970."

When the SQ took over from the RCMP in the region, the relationship didn't improve; Gilbert mentioned scenes of destruction during traditional ceremonies, reserve members being clubbed over the head; his defiance is still palpable.

"When I was young, for us the Sûreté was the devil. Still today, we have trouble making them understand the reality on the reserve, even if it has improved."

This also helps to explain the confrontational relationship between Laurie or Bryan and the provincial police. The SQ has been a colonial, repressive force; how to erase that image and the practices that likely still exist, and for how many more years to come? "When the Sûreté shows up on the reserve, people feel like they've already been clubbed over the head," Gilbert concluded.

*
* *
*

At least Kitigan Zibi's proximity means the residents of Maniwaki cannot overlook the country's First Peoples, which is the case in only a few regions of Quebec: the North Shore, Saguenay–Lac-Saint-Jean or Abitibi-Témiscamingue. In Quebec, self-identified Indigenous peoples make up only one percent of the population; for the most part, they live in isolated communities or far from urban centres, except for Kahnawake to the south, a stone's throw from Montreal; there is less Indigenous prostitution or homelessness in Montreal or Quebec City than in the big cities of the West. Over the months, I discovered the Québécois indifference to Indigenous peoples (even though the majority of descendants of French-Canadians have at least one Indigenous ancestor).[3] Their mood wavered between weariness over land claims and exasperation linked to the persistent social issues in First Peoples' communities. I've been told politely that it's an unpopular cause; at best, the subject elicits yawns.

What about murdered and missing Indigenous women? I was often told that all those murders happen out west, in Vancouver or on the Highway of Tears, not in this part of the country. So much for Maryse Fréchette (pregnant when she went missing in Joliette in 2007 at the age of seventeen), Sandra Gaudet (raped, tortured and strangled to death in Val d'Or in 1990 at the age of fourteen), Minnie Kenojuak (murdered in 1996), Bea Kwaronihawi Barnes (gone missing not far from Kahnawake in 2010 at seventeen), Evie Luuku (murdered in 1998 at thirty-nine), Kelly Morrisseau (pregnant, murdered in a Gatineau parking lot in 2006 at twenty-seven),

Tiffany Morrison (murdered in 2006 near Kahnawake at twenty-four), Ruby Ann Poucachiche (murdered in the Rouyn-Noranda region in 1999 at thirty-four), Leah Qavavauq (murdered in Montreal in 2005), Francesca Saint-Pierre (beaten to death in Montreal in 2007 at the age of fourteen), Jane Louise Sutherland (murdered in Gatineau in 1984 at twenty), Linda Condo (murdered on the Gaspé Peninsula in 1988), Ida Angotigirk (murdered in 2013 at forty-one), Marlène Barbeau (murdered in Limoilou in 2007 at forty-seven), and all the others.[4] So much for Shannon Alexander and Maisy Odjick. In May 2014, the RCMP estimated the number of Indigenous women murdered in Quebec between 1980 and 2012 at forty-six. That is 3 percent of women killed in the province,[5] even though they represent only one percent of all women living there. So, three times more likely to be a murder victim.

*
*   *
*

For the same demographic reasons—a smaller proportion of Indigenous people live in Quebec than in the western provinces—the province does not feel as affected by the history of Indian residential schools; there were only six[6] (out of approximately 130 in the country as a whole) and they "housed" "only" thirteen thousand children between 1948 and 1979 (as compared to 150,000 for all of Canada). But when the Truth and Reconciliation Commission travelled to Montreal in April 2013, Commissioner Marie Wilson reminded Quebec media that "the most active religious congregations in the management of residential schools were those found in Quebec." The Oblates, for example. In fact, it was through the residential schools—centres for abuse, family destruction and alienation from cultural identity—that violence took root in Indigenous communities. The "residential school syndrome"—difficulty loving oneself or loving or caring for others—is transmitted from one generation to the next, like a poison for which there is no antidote, and it can be traced and found in the stories of women murdered by those closest to them, in young chronic runaways and in alcoholic men exhibiting violent behaviour.

I attended excruciating "sharing sessions" organized by the Truth and Reconciliation Commission on residential schools, where it felt like I was hearing from the survivors of an internment camp. The room was full: the audience, Indigenous for the most part, in tears, myself included. Tissues were methodically distributed by women who then returned with wastepaper baskets to recover the sodden remains. A man from Kitigan Zibi spoke of his years at residential school, starting when he was four: the four rapes he remembered, the blows to his head delivered by nuns, mostly because he wasn't learning French quickly enough. And his life of despair and alcoholism, his inability to raise his children, his many attempts at suicide. Others told of the grip of hunger and thirst, sometimes daily sexual violence committed by those in charge of the residential school, and of bunk-mates who committed suicide; some witnesses didn't see their parents for years at a time. Each man and woman described the same devastating impact on their lives and those of their children. The residential school syndrome is a direct—though not the sole—cause of the phenom-enon of missing and murdered women; it made entire communities vulnerable. The commission revealed that at least 4,134 children died in residential schools from untreated illnesses, abuse, suicide, accidents during attempts to flee, even from starvation. We are told that this is only a provisional number.

Gilbert estimated that some one hundred living members of Kitigan Zibi attended residential schools, either Pointe-Bleue in Quebec or the Spanish Indian Residential School in Ontario. "The priest, the Indian agent or the police would suggest a residential school to the poorest families, telling them their children would be well fed, receive warm clothing. Clothing that was taken away sometimes as soon as they arrived at the school." With his innate streak of intellectual honesty, remembering a colleague who went to residential school as a teen and received an education from quality educa-tors, he added, "Some didn't have too bad an experience there." The 150-year history of the residential school policy (1830–1990), poorly taught in schools and little known by the Canadian public, resurfaces in unexpected places. For example, in words spoken by an Anglophone high school math teacher in Maniwaki in May 2014.

Rowdy pupils from the Algonquin community of Barrier Lake[7] were told to "go back to residential school to learn manners and discipline." She later apologized.

*
* *
*

Shaken by Maisy and Shannon's disappearance, Chief Whiteduck continues to fight for the families of missing and murdered Indigenous women. He even presented a motion to the Assembly of First Nations for Quebec and Labrador, eastern Canada's Indigenous government, to create a special team to help communities that have seen members disappear. The motion didn't carry, but Gilbert himself went to Manawan, an Attikamek reserve in Quebec, to lend a hand after one such disappearance. On May 12, 2014, when demonstrators interrupted a public relations exercise for the federal justice minister on the steps of Parliament to demand a national inquiry on missing and murdered women, brandishing an urn containing a young woman's ashes, Gilbert was in the thick of the action with the other demonstrators, all women, taking a stand in his own calm, determined way.

He thinks that one day someone will speak out. Someone will say what they know about Shannon and Maisy's disappearance. "One day, the earlier the better."

Before colonization, Algonquin peoples from the region gathered every summer along the banks of the Desert River—not far from the place where *Pakwaun* hockey games are played. Above the hockey players and the frozen river, a green footbridge leads to Maniwaki's high school.

Early on the evening of September 5, 2008, Maisy and Shannon made their way to a dance there, at the *Poly*.

16
PITOBIG STREET, KITIGAN ZIBI
September 5, 2008

I had fallen into the habit of coming in from the north via the Laurentian highway. I couldn't seem to bring myself to change my route; driving down the highway lulled me into a needed state of suspension, of emptiness, five whole hours during which I could listen and try to understand. For a long time, I didn't realize that, had I driven in from the south, the Ottawa side, I would have been greeted by a huge billboard/missing persons poster of the two girls, made possible by a fundraising effort. This is how one enters the reserve, under the gaze of Shannon—her cadet version, beret and all—and Maisy—smiling, her hair pulled back; passing to the left of their faces, weathered by the elements. I don't know if this book would have turned out differently, if I would have felt even more haunted.

I imagined their parents and grandparents returning from Ottawa after a day's shopping or visiting friends,

hands on the steering wheel, driving past the large billboard. Does it tear them apart every time? For the space
of a few minutes, do they try to step outside of the land-
scape, of reality? Do they whisper prayers?

Do they make of this moment a silent dialogue with
their missing loved one?

> *hey there girl!!! we all worried about you . . .
> just let us know that you're ok!! (P, September
> 10) • send a shout out 2 let us know ur ok (A,
> September 10) • MAISY, COME HOME!!
> PLEASE!! (D, September 13) • maisey! let me
> know your ok! give me a call you know my num-
> ber (K, September 13) • Maisy! where are you
> man? i miss you, plz come back. everybody's
> worried (M, September 14) • Maisy, please let
> anyone know you are okay . . . we're missing
> you lots! love you (M, September 15) • Maisy!!!
> please come home safee!!! ilu gurrrll, *Lala
> Princesses forever!!* (N, September 18).*†

"The last time I saw Maisy. . ." Maria pondered, "I'm
not sure. But I think it was in the spring, four months
before she went missing. She came to spend a week with
me in Ottawa. She was really nice, babysat my kids, took

---

† These messages and the others that follow were posted on Maisy's
Facebook wall over the course of the months after she went missing.
Laurie Odjick kindly gave permission to reprint them here. Messages to
Shannon are no longer accessible.

them to Tim Hortons . . . I even remember she loaned me $40 when it was me who was supposed to be looking after her!"

Maria smiled.

"The last time I saw Maisy," her father, Rick, wrote to me, "was at John's funeral, my sister Maria's partner . . ."

"The last time I saw them . . ." Laurie recalled, "I dropped by my mom's place and she was with Shannon mowing Mom's lawn and laughing, joking around. Maisy kissed me and said, 'Love you, Mom, talk to you later!' and I left. I didn't notice anything out of the ordinary."

"The last time I saw them . . ." Lisa said, "I was at home on the afternoon of September 5, 2008. They slept over and were mowing my lawn. They needed money to go to a dance at the high school, and my husband paid them to cut the grass. Then they left the house on my old rickety bike with Shannon sitting on the back."

Lisa laughed; she could still *see* the gleeful wobbing pair as they started on the seven-kilometre trip to Maniwaki.

"The last time I saw them . . ." Maisy's brother Damon remembered, "It was the day before they went missing around eight at night. I was out biking and they were hanging with friends on Main Street in front of the old Central Hotel. "

"The last time I saw them . . ." Bryan said, "It was Saturday, September 6. The girls slept at my house. I left to catch a bus to Ottawa around noon. Shannon walked me there, and I gave her a bit of money for the weekend."

Maisy! 12 days of pure torture! please let us know your ok!! (S, September 18) • maisy! call home to at least say your still alive . . . everyones really worried . . . do you know how much your hurting your family & friends by leaving and not letting anyone know whether your dead or alive? call home! (R, September 19) • hey maze iam realy crying everybody is plz call or let us know you're safe plzz call (A, September 20)

Laurie and I left the café shortly before eleven on the morning of January 11, 2014. She was wearing light spring shoes at a time when all of Quebec was covered in ice. Laughing, she clung to my arm and we made our cautious way to her car. She was taking me to see the area around the *polyvalente*—the name still used at times to describe public high schools—a collection of brick buildings that reminded me of my *lycée* in France. It's where the girls went on the evening of Friday the 5th for the school dance. We stared at the benches, the lawns covered in snow.

"I don't know where they were during the squabble," Laurie said. "Maybe here by the bridge? Who knows."

Cousins and acquaintances told police the girls showed up at the dance drunk, they had taken out their piercings and claimed they'd smoked crack. Shortly afterwards, they were kicked out. Once outside, Shannon got into an argument with Maisy's cousin, pushing him up against a wall and tearing his shirt.

The *polyvalente*, the school in Maniwaki, where Maisy and Shannon were seen at a dance the evening before their disappearance.

Soon afterward both girls left together.

Next, Laurie dropped me off at Bryan's former apartment on Koko Street, a small two-storey building, red on the bottom half, white on the top, sitting next to a playground. I took a few guarded pictures of the apartment; the new tenants watched me through the window. I wanted to follow in the girls' footsteps from the apartment, where they would have put on their make-up, got dressed, then left for the high school. Witnesses saw them making their way there on foot.

It was late on a Saturday morning, the street corner was deserted and the road so slippery that I had to walk down the middle on gravel that a city truck had just spread. Maniwaki was a dingy white and not yet fully awake. A few residents swept snow from their roofs. I kept going, crossed Odjick Street (Lisa didn't know which Odjick the street had been named after, several long-time reserve residents have the same name). Damon told me he saw Maisy on Main Street, which meant they detoured before the dance—maybe they hadn't taken the green bridge spanning the river like I did, with its view of the school.

What did they talk about as they walked through the small charmless town? Did they dream of escape, of growing up even faster? Were they excited about the upcoming dance? Did they hope to hook up, have some fun?

> *Maze plzz come home or at least call some-*
> *one im like so freking upset right now they*
> *had a little ceremony @ school the other day*
> *for you and Shannon, your sister, your mom,*
> *your grandma. Everyone is worried sick. wes*
> *all misses you a bunch. plzz call eyes crying for*
> *you i misses you a lot girl plzz call me i'm sickin*
> *tired because i miss you to much i cant stop*
> *thinking about where you are and what you are*

doing. What is going through your mind like right now youve got every body driven crazy out of their minds back here. we miss you and you have a lot of love back here everyone is just waiting for that one phone call maz plzz call soon ASAP plzz xoxo love (S, September 23) • Hey Maze, We Miss You And I Tink Its Time 4 U 2 Cum Back. Lik Maze Your Mom Really Loves You. Shit Happened Between Yous But Everyone Has Problems. Its Okay Now Just Come Home Man. Lik Everyone's Worried Sick (M, September 26) •mais man, me n dd went n put flyers up today, its all over the city man, everyone knows now . . . everyone misses you, and ppl are saying that they seen you on vanier in ottawa? C'mon man . . . come back plzz we miss you soo much!! xoxo lotss of love! (M, September 29).

When Maria filled out the forms on Shannon for the Missing Children Society, she wrote the following as dictated by Bryan: "Bryan waited 24 hours before he reported her missing to police because he thought that was procedure." In fact, Bryan and Lisa called police on Tuesday, September 9, the day after they met and discovered the girls' wallets and belongings. Bryan contacted the SQ in Maniwaki, and Lisa contacted Kitigan Zibi's police services.

The lag between the assumed time of their disappearance and the alert sounded by the families has been waved about as an excuse any time the police's efforts have been called into question. By the police services themselves—"They had a good start on us," argued Gordon McGregor. And by the editorialist from the *Ottawa Citizen,* who saw the lag linked to a social component: "From the outset, it would become clear that this case had its own unique and difficult characteristics, the first sign being that it would be four days before anyone called the police. . . . The fact that many days passed before their disappearance was reported is symbolic of the disadvantages that the girls faced, probably from the time they were born, in trying to get a fair shake at a decent life. If this is a story about social inequality, then it's a story that begins long before the girls went missing."[1] Some pointed out that, in contrast, police were alerted the next day by the parents of young Brandon, the video-game addict runaway.[2]

But those "four days" were actually only three—perhaps even fewer. Maisy and Shannon were seen for the last time by Bryan on Saturday, September 6, around noon. He got home from Ottawa sooner than expected the next day at about 5 p.m. It is impossible to know exactly when they disappeared over the barely thirty intervening hours. Saturday night. Or Sunday morning.

"My mom called me on Sunday at noon, worried she hadn't heard from Maisy, even though she'd tried to call her several times at the apartment," Laurie told me. "I was working at Home Hardware that day. There was no reason to worry yet. I said, 'Mom, they're teens . . . Either they're still asleep or they're over at friends . . . ' On Monday I still hoped they'd show up. But maybe I was in denial by then," she added.

Sure, Bryan could have started to worry as soon as he got back on Sunday evening; sure, the alert could have been sounded on Monday. That would mean a lag time of twenty-four hours, not four days. The lag was mostly the police's doing, their failure to react promptly when the famous red flags went up—all the signs suggesting the girls did not leave the apartment of their own accord—their failure to examine the clues in the apartment properly. The comparison with Brandon Crisp is irrelevant. When the fifteen-year-old Ontario boy decided to run away from home because his Xbox had been confiscated, his father helped him pack his bag as a way of teaching him a lesson: go on your little journey, I understand your anger, something like that. He had no idea his son would actually run away; he had good reason to worry when there was no sign of his son the day after his departure.

What would people have said about Laurie or Bryan if they had helped their daughters pack their bags and run away?

Adolescents and the silences they keep. The mystery they shroud entire chapters of their life in. The anguish you try to muzzle when night falls and your child has not answered the phone. The mounting anxiety, interspersed with moments of respite. The fear of calling police for nothing. Non-Indigenous parents could probably have convinced journalists there was genuine cause for worry and explained why they had waited before taking action. It's more difficult when you live on a reserve.

When the disappearance was made public, Kitigan Zibi's administration gave Laurie three days off. Then she returned to her job as a radio host on the reserve. How were you able to pretend that nothing had happened; did you say anything on air? I asked her. "No, I didn't talk on air about the girls. It's so emotional for me. The ladies that also worked there, they did the announcing for the girls."

Awh Maisy . . . I Miss You . . . I Really Need You, And You Aren't Even Around 2 Talk To • I Weally Hope Your OK Maze . . . You Might Not Even Be Able To C This, But It Makes Me Feel Better Writing To You • I R Lovest You Maisy 4Ever My Best Friend Forever • Love • Please Come Home Safe (R, October 3) • Mais . . . Come please come home i miss you soo much, everyone is worried sick . . . please call okay please xoxo lots of love . . . again (M, October 7) • MAISY!! JUST CALL SOMEONE!!! WE WON'T BE MAD!!! WE NEED TO KNOW YOUR OKAY!!! PLEASE! EVERYONE UP HERE IS ASKING ABOUT YOU!! IT'S TO HARD TO HOLD IN

MY TEARS!! JUST TELL US UR OKAY!! oops caps lock . . . (S, October 18) • maisy let someone know that your okay everyone misses you alot and everyone just wants to know that nothing bads happened to you (S, October 22).

My favourite missing person notice is the one published jointly by the Ontario Provincial Police and the SQ, probably sometime during the winter of 2008–09. Both girls are shown, and the person who came up with the design published two photos for each girl instead of just one. That was one of the recommendations made by Maryanne Pearce in her thesis. From experience, thinking of her own daughter, she observed that teenagers often change their hairstyle. It makes no sense to use only one picture to help the public identify a missing girl.

So we see both a stunning Maisy, her hair pulled back and piercings in both corners of her mouth and in her nostril, and Maisy the mischievous tomboy with short hair; as for Shannon, we see a beautiful girl, chin held high and forehead bare in the picture on the left, and on the right, a silent film star with bangs. Another poster includes five different pictures of Shannon—a tired-looking young girl with a forced smile; a cadet sporting a beret, her gaze intent; with short hair; tanned; and with bangs again; she is amazingly different from one picture to the next. We see the elasticity of teenaged faces, we get a sense of how much the day's mood colours their features, we appreciate how the pictures pay homage to the two young girls' multiplicity. They're not carved from one same block; they cannot be reduced, for example, to their Indigenous origins or their liking for marijuana.

If I am grateful for the missing persons posters, despite their grim look and the sinister file numbers shown (20080216 and 20080215, but also 2012020142 depending on the police department), it is because they bear witness to Maisy and Shannon's existence; that they have, or had, a body, clothes, special marks and so are prevented from becoming ghosts. When she went missing, Shannon had scars on her left knee, pierced ears and navel; her skin was "pockmarked" and she had pimples; she wore a silver necklace with a feather on it. We read that she spoke both English and French and, according to the posters, was either 5 foot 8, 5 foot 9 or 5 foot 10; the last time she was seen, she was wearing "red and white Asics running shoes." As for Maisy, she had "piercings on her bottom lip and left nostril, and scars on top of her right eyebrow and left forearm and another piercing on her sternum; she wore black capris and a green T-shirt; according to the notices, she measured 5 foot 10 or 6 foot and spoke only English.

> *Happy 17th Birthday Maisy ... I hope somehow, someway you can read this and see how many care and love you ... Miss you and Love you so*

*much! (M, November 6) • Happy Birthday LiL
miss Maisy . . . Love ya miss ya cant wait to hug
n kiss ya!!! (L, November 7)*

Shannon and Maisy came home after their evening
had been cut short, quite likely angry at being kicked
out, maybe still drunk. They went to bed, Shannon in
her room and Maisy on the living room couch. When
Shannon walked Bryan to the bus stop around noon,
Maisy was still asleep.

And then.

What happened?

A known marijuana dealer from the reserve called
them several times over the course of the afternoon.

Maisy spent a long time on the phone with friends
from the Saugeen region, her stepfather's community in
Ontario.

Neighbours heard the sounds of a small party that
night.

That is all I know.

I also read the following on the Missing Children
Society form that Maria filled out according to Bryan's
dictation:

> *Gang X:[3] Shannon fought with a guy from this
> gang/rumors were that Shannon was scared/
> ages in gang are 14-24/ Natives vs. non-Natives/
> X was stabbed by one of the gang members in
> the past year.*

X: wrote something funny/weird on [Shannon's] Facebook wall/ was the last person to call Shannon/ she won't answer phone now.

X: his story changed many times on when was the last time he talked with Maisy and/or Shannon.

The gang mentioned in the first paragraph is a group of white youth from Maniwaki.

The alleged guests at the small party, two young men from the reserve, were questioned by police.

Nothing came of the questioning.

According to police, every lead was explored—although badly and too late. A former RCMP officer volunteered to carry out an investigation on behalf of the Missing Children Society and, once he'd finished, he told Maria, "I feel like I know even less now than when I started."

It was as though the girls had swept away every last trace, then climbed up on their broom and flown away.

An SQ investigator is still on the case. Maybe one day, as Gilbert hopes, someone will talk.

*
 *   *
 *

Happy 17th birthday, my girl, we love you and miss you . . . Your sister wanted a cake and candles. So tonight we're celebrating your birthday.

They miss you and ask for you every day. Call Grandma, that's all you have to do, we just want to hear your voice and know you're alright. Just a phone call . . . Please . . . I love you so much. Your Family (November 6).

*

*   *

*

The last time I went to Kitigan Zibi, I left the reserve driving south. I turned around to look at the girls on the billboard. I would have loved to meet them. Their lanky silhouettes and their appetite for life haunt the streets of Kitigan Zibi and Maniwaki still.

Where are they.

Epilogue

This book was published in Quebec and France in November 2014. Since that time, there have been some new developments regarding certain protagonists. Below is an update for a few of them as of March 2015.

Maria Jacko, Maisy's aunt, decided to redouble her efforts to shed light on the disappearance of her niece and Shannon. She wrote me that, "Maisy and Shannon are on my mind a lot lately and I want to do more to find them. I want to meet with my friends and show all the clues I have and do something from there."

Laurie Odjick, Maisy's mom, was designated to represent the Quebec families during the Round Table on Missing and Murdered Women held on February 27, 2015. She continues to work towards establishing a foundation for families, Maisy's Foundation of Hope.

Gilbert Whiteduck, the chief of Kitigan Zibi's band council, has decided to leave his position after six very intense years. His decision is linked to health issues but is connected to Maisy and Shannon's disappearance as well. Below is what he told me over the phone. "I was elected as chief the year they disappeared . . . I feel that I did everything I could do, and we still don't have any definitive information, nothing to answer the two families' questions. It's very discouraging. It made me want to become involved in the #MMIW cause, but differently. The failure of the February 27th Round Table confirms my desire to go ahead with initiatives without waiting for federal support. I hope to volunteer with Quebec Native Women and the Assembly of First Nations of Quebec and Labrador (AFNQL) around the issue. I would like to work toward finding tools to help families and communities affected by these disappearances."

Michèle Audette has left the presidency of the Native Women's Association of Canada. She has become active in federal politics in the hope of being elected to Parliament to continue defending the cause of Indigenous women.

Afterword
Final Thoughts from Laurie Odjick
Friday, April 17, 2015

On whether the Canadian public is paying more attention to the issue of MMIW . . .

I think there's been more awareness raised on the issue. I think what got us back out there was when they found Tina [Fontaine]. It's sad that it takes something like that to wake people up . . . the fact that there are so many missing Aboriginal girls out there. But as for what we want as families, nothing has changed. We are all really grateful just to get the awareness out there, but what some families want from the government just is not happening. You hear Harper and his comments, and he forgets that we're reading those things as families, and it honestly sounds like he really doesn't care. That's hurtful and frustrating and also maddening at the same time, because we don't feel like our girls are valued as human beings that way. And so awareness is great, but we need to see action done for our families.

On the statistic mentioned by Minister of Aboriginal Affairs Bernard Valcourt at a meeting with First Nations leaders, and later confirmed by the RCMP, that 70 percent of murdered Indigenous women are killed by Indigenous men . . .

I think the government wants to shift the blame and the focus off of themselves. They're not doing much. Valcourt is there to work with our people and for our people, and he is absolutely not doing that, making statements like that. How dare he make that assumption? And that's what I call it. To me it's just a big diversion for them. And it just puts more anger in the Aboriginal community for him to say things like that. And that's what he wants. He wants people to get angry. Then he can say, "See, there you go. There it is." "Watch," I said, "the media is going to grab at this real quick." And it happened.

On how bias can influence information . . .

People living different lifestyles do put some of themselves at risk. There's no denying that. But for Maisy, right away the police and the media wanted to say that she had a risky lifestyle. No, she didn't! But yet they so quickly wanted to put her in that category. That really pissed me off. She was a typical teenager. It was sad because I had to watch what I was saying to media. And that's the question that they always asked me. When they found out Maisy was living with her grandma, they'd ask, "What kind of problems were at home?" Maisy just didn't like my rules.

On speaking to her other children about Maisy . . .

They live it every day. There's not much to say to them. They don't have their sister here with them, and that's what we deal with as a family. People out there are not very nice sometimes. There is a meanness, and that's what we deal with as a family.

On what we should be telling young women about how to live their lives and about the choices they make . . .

For me, I think I would like them to take a step back and to really look at their situation. Life is hard. Life is cruel. And there's not-nice people out there, and people will take advantage. And so basically I think they need to take a step back and really look at the world around them before they either decide to run away or take off. Be vigilant about your surroundings. There are so many things that I would like to tell them, when the girls go out and—buddy system and all those things—but to me I have a hard time with that because everybody's situation is different. There are some teenagers that leave their homes for very valid reasons, so I cannot say, "stay home." They can make safe choices. And that's all it is. Be safe.

On what she would like to say to the Canadian public . . .

Our girls are not what the media and other people perceive them to be. Stay away from that. No matter what lifestyle they're living, these women belong to loving families who care for them. They are loved and they are valued. And we miss them. And all we want for our loved ones is justice, just like anybody else would want for their family if something happened to them.

Acknowledgements

A very special thank you to Laurie Odjick, Lisa Odjick, Mark Roote, Rick Jacko, Damon Jacko, Maria Jacko, Bryan Alexander, Gilbert Whiteduck, Gordon McGregor; a thank you to the beyond to Pamela Sickles, Shannon's grandmother, who died on May 22, 2014, never knowing what happened to her granddaughter.

Huge thanks to Maryanne Pearce, whose work and generosity are exceptional; to Brendan Kennedy, for his receptiveness, his kindness and the quality of his articles on Maisy and Shannon.

Thank you to Michèle Audette and Lorna Martin of the Native Women's Association of Canada, and to the whole gang from Quebec Native Women—including Viviane Michel, Widia Larivière, Aurélie Arnaud, Alana Boileau and Josiane Loiselle-Bourdeau. Thank you to Craig Benjamin, Karine Gentelet and Béatrice Vaugrante from Amnesty International.

Thank you to Sylvain Lafrance and Georges Lafontaine from Maniwaki, Val Napoleon from the

University of Victoria, Alex Smale of Statistics Canada, Jean-Marie David from the Special Committee on Violence Against Indigenous Women, Melanie Morrison from Kahnawake, Bridget Tolley from Families of Sisters in Spirit, Maya Rolbin-Ghanie from Missing Justice, Audrey Huntley from No More Silence and David Falls from the Royal Canadian Mounted Police.

Thank you to Vida Dardachti, Éva Kyziridès, Sonia Martin, Kate Battle and Larissa Hallis for their assistance in ways big and small in retranscribing and translating for the original French edition of this book.

Thank you to my editor, Alexandre Sánchez, to Mireille Paolini and to David Dufresne for everything and more, and to Rémi Leroux, astute photographer; to my wonderful translators, Susan Ouriou and Christelle Morelli, and to Jennifer Lambert, who has made it possible for this book to travel into English.

Finally, thank you to Dépanneur Café and to those who never ceased to encourage me: Ginette Viens, Benoît Roy, Judith Rouan, Eric and Colette Walter.

Thank you Ju, Jo and Gus.

Thank you! *Migwech!*

Appendices

March 8, 2009

To whom it may concern:

I write this letter to you as a concerned mother and citizen. I would like to bring to your attention several issues concerning the disappearance of my daughter, Maisy Odjick, and the manner in which the Kitigan Zibi Police Services (KZPS) and the Sûreté du Québec have handled this case. Since my daughter's disappearance, September 6, 2008, to the present day, very little to nil support and communication has been provided by these police services. The lack of police services and support from the onset has been a long, frustrating and exhausting six months for me and my family.

My sixteen-year-old daughter was not alone when

she disappeared. She and her friend Shannon Alexander (seventeen years old) were together, and both disappeared on September 6, 2008. I am deeply concerned for Shannon's whereabouts, but out of respect for Shannon's father and family, I cannot nor am I speaking for her in this letter.

I am of the position that government authorities, agencies and the public need to be informed on the incompetent, unprofessional, uncooperative, unaccountable behaviour of police services, in particular, the Kitigan Zibi Police Services (herein referred to as KZPS). In addition, as a community member of the Kitigan Zibi Anishnabeg (herein referred to as KZA), I am also unsatisfied with the Chief and Council's lack of leadership in directing concrete action and demanding accountability from the police concerning my daughter's case. The lack of support, transparency and accountability is unacceptable. As you can appreciate, the disappearance of your child speaks volumes of worries, immense feelings of loss, isolation, heartache, mental anguish, and extreme emotional pain. I live with these emotions every minute of each day.

I demand my right to services, justice and support in locating my daughter. I have been exercising my rights all along. However, I feel as though I do not have the right to exercise my right to information concerning my *minor* daughter. For instance; when I called the Sûreté du Québec to speak to a police officer investigating the Shannon Alexander case, I was informed to speak to the

Kitigan Zibi police services because the Sûreté do not have my file, and I am not related to Shannon. I understand the nature of confidentiality; however, where else can I turn for police information when in fact I receive nil to no information from the KZPS. And, when I do receive any information from the KZPS, it is very skeleton and unprofessional in nature.

Furthermore, the police only provided information after much persistence on my part. My demand for reports is a very time-consuming and overwhelming task. For example; since September 2008, I have received only one report. It took me two months, from December 2008 to February 2009, after constant requests to the KZA Chief and Council. Just recently, I received a report. This report is eight double-spaced pages in length with no letterhead or signature. It should be noted that in reading the report, I am left with the feeling that I did the police's job because they report on leads and sources which I provided to this police service. In the end, there is nothing substantial. Once again, I am left with much more questions, uncertainty and emptiness.

It must be noted that at the onset of Maisy's and Shannon's disappearance, no thorough ground search or proper investigation was conducted. At this point, any evidence collected in September 2008 is damaged because the police that collected the evidence did not possess the expertise to do so. Furthermore, the families were not given any information on the results of the evidence collected.

Very recently, a media source informed me that the Sûreté du Québec have evidence that indicates the girls ran away. If this is true, why has not the KZ police service or the band council informed me of this? If this is true, then is the file closed? If this is true, does this resolve my daughter's disappearance? A number of questions still remain: where is my daughter and what resources will be made available to find her, and what evidence was used to make this conclusion? I demand and deserve no less to be informed and provided with this evidence or any information pursuant to this case.

Since my daughter's disappearance, I have been asking for answers to my numerous inquiries. I have been demanding a full and proper investigation. I have been requesting a full report which is inclusive of sound actions taken and end results. I have been demanding continual communication with the police services. My inquiries and demands have not been answered in a respectful and satisfactory manner. Since September 2008, I have been asking for an answer to two very simple but monumental questions: **WHY WAS MY DAUGHTER'S FILE TRANSFERRED TO THE KITIGAN ZIBI POLICE SERVICES BY THE SÛRETÉ DU QUÉBEC? WHO GAVE THIS ORDER?** I cannot help but feel that there is a cover up here.

I cannot understand why this occurred, in light of the fact that Maisy was not on the reserve when she disappeared. In looking at this situation, on the one hand, an argument can be made that the decision was made because of a jurisdictional issue; however, on the other hand, in a legal context, where the harm occurred, then this is the jurisdiction to deal with the matter. In my daughter's case, her disappearance is the harm, and the disappearance happened while she was off reserve, therefore, the Sûreté du Québec is the proper policy authority to conduct the investigation and handle the case. I do not wish for my daughter to become a jurisdictional issue, nor to be immediately ruled as a "runaway" teen. These are lame excuses used to negate the seriousness of this situation, to deny support and resources, to default on action, to discriminate against me and my daughter, to refuse responsibility and to be accountable to the people. This is unacceptable to me as a human being, a mother, as a member of the community, and a citizen of society.

In essence, I feel that both the KZPS and KZA have applied the standard practice of blaming the victim. I am the victim, but to these entities, it is my fault that Maisy ran away; it is my fault that she disappeared; it is my fault that I waited too long to inform the police; it is my fault that I do not contact the police regularly by way of phone calls or station visits.

Is it my fault that I am demanding answers, accountability and actions to be taken by both entities? To treat my daughter's disappearance as a "runaway" teen; or to treat her as promiscuous, and to treat me as the faulting party is abominably unacceptable. I feel that justice is denied. A young girl is missing. I urgently demand that action by the proper authorities must be taken to find her. I demand that the proper police authority take all and necessary steps to help locate my daughter. My daughter deserves support and justice as any other missing person, for instance; Brandon Crisp, Ardeth Woods, Jennifer Teague.

It does not make sense that the KZ police service and the KZA community leaders invested so much time, financial resources and media attention to locate a missing lion cub, but nil to nothing is invested for our missing young girls. How much money was spent on finding Boomer, the baby lion? Maisy and Shannon are community members; they are also citizens of society and they deserve attention, support and justice.

My daughter's return home, or at the very least, to know her whereabouts; to know what happened to her are my main priorities and it is with urgency that I call upon your office to assist me in acquiring from the Sûreté du Québec, Kitigan Zibi Police Services and the Kitigan Zibi Anishinabeg Chief and Council prompt, professional and unequivocal answers to all my inquiries; to obtain a full and proper investigation of Maisy's disappearance, with the appropriate expertise to be employed; and for the Kitigan Zibi police services and Kitigan Zibi Anishinabeg Chief and Council to be held accountable to me, my family and to the people for their inability to demonstrate due diligence in accountability and transparency with my daughter's case.

Should you like to discuss the contents of my letter,

please do not hesitate to contact me at justiceformissing @gmail.com. I look forward to hearing from your office concerning the issues I raised in this letter. I thank you for your attention and kind consideration to my letter.

Sincerely,

Laurie Odjick

CONNIE GREYEYES' SPEECH ON PARLIAMENT HILL
OCTOBER 4, 2013

I bring to you the stories of my cousin, my auntie, and my friends, who are loved and missed. In 2008, my good friend Dave told me about the SIS vigils that were happening. He was so excited he said, we have to do one. So I agreed. Tonight we're holding our sixth vigil in Fort St. John, B.C. Unfortunately, after the first vigil my friend passed away, and he's here with me today, as a brother in spirit. It wasn't up until recently that I realized that I've always been surrounded by this violence that has happened, and my story is not unique. Many of us have several friends and family members that are missing.

The first one that comes to mind is Florence of Fort St. John, British Columbia. She was my good friend's great-grandmother and my friend's mother. She was murdered in 1965 and dumped on the side of the road like a piece of garbage. When the man went to Court he got two years less a day, he served eighteen months and was released. He actually had a judge . . . one of her daughters told me that a judge actually went in and spoke in the Courts for him, told what a good man he was.

I remember when I was about eight years old, we used to go and visit this beautiful woman. Her name was Sandra Calahasen. I remember she was so pretty and she reminded me of Priscilla Presley. And I remember just thinking what a beautiful girl, I hope that I will look like that when I'm older. She was found dumped on 101 B.C. The person that was accused of doing this to her was charged with tampering with a dead body.

The next one is . . . when I was a teenager and I befriended this wonderful girl, she was just a take-no-shit, just an awesome fun person to be around, we did all sorts of crazy things. She went missing in 1988. Her name is Stacey Rogers. And she is missed and loved, and we wonder where she is.

In 1993 my family had always been friends with this fiery redhead. She was so tough she just kicked ass all the time, her name was Ramona Jean Shuler. She's not been seen since November of 1993. And she is one of the main reasons that I started this vigil in Fort St. John. Because I miss my redhead friend. She was beautiful, she had children who miss her. I see pictures of her daughter on Facebook, and her daughter's daughter, and I wonder if she sees those too . . . You know, what a tragic loss . . . Where is she??

At the same time in 1993, my beautiful cousin Joyce Cardinal was murdered in Edmonton. She was beaten and doused with gasoline. And when the police came they thought it was a rubbish fire, because the flames were five feet high. He just left her to die. My woman warrior cousin didn't die until twenty-two days later in the hospital. Recently I went to my community and I visited my auntie. And I remember looking at her thinking, I wonder if she remembers, she's starting to lose her memory now and I was thinking, it's horrible to think that, that might be a good thing that you don't remember that happening to your daughter. You don't remember that somebody just beat her up and lit her on fire and left her to die.

As the days moved into 1994, a strong Dane-zaa woman named Molly Apsassin was walking in her community in Doig River First Nation. Somebody just randomly shot her and killed her. He was ordered out of Doig River First Nation and never to return again.

In 2005, I learned of a young woman missing. Her name was Rene Gunning. I befriended her father Joe. She had a son named D'Andre . . . he'd always been a supporter of the vigils that we started. And I remember the year he was gone to have to declare her legally dead. They had found her just prior to our vigil. And I was asked to come to his house and sit with him and his fiancée. And I remember him talking as we smudged and prayed and drummed. You know . . . She had a son! He doesn't have his mother now. And how . . . how are you supposed to feel now that they found her? She wasn't alone, she was with Krystle Knott, who she went missing with. But it's almost a relief that she was not by herself that night.

These are all women that are missing from Fort St. John, B.C., a small community. The following year my good friend Shirley Clethroe went missing. The family assumed she had gone to one friend's or her other sister's and it was not until seven days later that they were able to legally report her missing. And it wasn't until she missed a court date, that the police said okay, now in 48 hours, you can report her missing. Her daughter was on these steps here last year, and I bring the story here with me. Cause she was a good friend of mine and I miss her.

In May 2008, Annie Davis was murdered in Chetwynd, not far from Fort St. John; her family resides in and around Fort St. John. She is a member of the Apsassin family who also had a member of their family murdered, Molly, the one that was shot down in Doig River.

In 2010, Cynthia Maas, who was also another member of the Apsassin family, was found murdered in Prince George, B.C. She was the alleged victim of Cody Legebokoff and I think he is supposed to stand trial in September of 2013.

In 2010, my beloved Aunt Nora at eighty-seven years old was struck down by a mobile treatment centre. If you don't know what that is, it is like an ambulance for rigs and pipelines. Three people were in the vehicle when they ran her over. And they jumped out and seen her laying on the ground with my uncle who was right there and had seen it all and they chose to get in the vehicle and drive away. They chose to leave an elder, run over, to die.

You know . . . talking to my uncle after that . . . and the person that ended up running her over was a family friend. And the police told us that if he doesn't admit it, he will never get a conviction. So I wrote, I videotaped a message to him. I said, "This was my auntie that you ran over and last year you were marching up Main Street in Fort St. John with us, drumming to end violence and find justice for our women." And he did the right thing. And he got two years for running her over. The other two people that were in the vehicle, one was a medic, never, never had any repercussions. She went on to have her medic business . . . Because in Canada, it's not a crime to leave the scene of a crime, even if that person is killed, if you were not the driver.

There's another girl that's missing in Fort St. John and I understand that her family is about to attend their first vigil in Fort St. John. She's been missing since 2010 and her name was Abigail Andrews. She was pregnant when she went missing. And my heart is in Fort St. John this evening because I know that this must be a really hard thing that they gonna have to go through tonight.

As I was writing down what I had to say, I felt sad that I even had to write it down, so that I can remember all these women from Fort St. John that are missing. And nobody seems to care! You know . . . how many marches and vigils and rallies do we have to go to before they go, "What's going on here?"

This is a community of, like, eighteen to twenty thousand when there's work in the winter! Why are so many women missing? I just started weeping. And it brought me back to the night when somebody tried to grab me. I was walking and I remember that night there was a meteor shower, and he followed me down the street and I remember in my gut I felt it, I knew something was gonna happen and I was scared. I kept on walking and I turned down the road to go to my mother's house. And he tried to cut me off. And he grabbed my arm and then with my other hand I slammed him in the nose and I just ran. And when I called the police and tried to report it, I was crying uncontrollably. And they dismissed me. Just like all these families have been dismissed. There was no, "Are you okay?" "Do you remember anything?" No follow-up phone call. I was just another Aboriginal person. Another Aboriginal woman, you know, she shouldn't have been walking at night because . . . you know . . . Not my right to walk around at night in B.C.

So in closing I would like to read a poem that my niece Helen Knott wrote in honour of missing and murdered women.

Invisible

Your eyes
they curve
around me.
I watch you try so hard
to find your way
past me.

Your sight is like rushing waters
moving
beside me,
behind me,

pushing over me,
indirectly consuming me.

They say
the path of least resistance
makes rivers and men crooked.

I am here.
I have resisted.
I am resisting.
I did not make you crooked.

What is it about you
structural giants?
What is it about your
pockmarked protection?
What is it about your
false perceptions?

What beliefs
have you bound to my body?
What pathologies
have you painted the pigment of my skin?
What bad medicine
did your forefathers use
to make me
invisible?

You don't want to see me.
What's worse is that you have the choice

whether or not
you see me.

I become a casualty of your blindness.
Subjected to your one-sided
absent-mindedness
because you've been given a privilege
called selective vision.
You weed out the colours
that don't match your peripheral preference,
and I am not part of your rainbow,
your twisted-light promises
for better tomorrows.

My face can be plastered on posters
telling you what
I was last seen wearing,
with fitted descriptions,
a location to give you bearings,
and you can choose
to look past me,
and go on,
uncaring.

My raven's hair and heritage
does not sound
alarm bells.
It does not stir you
to look for me.
Because

you have never
really
seen me.

You've seen me all right.
You've seen me on street corners,
lips red like sirens,
dreams broken like
sidewalk syringes,
neurotic like Catholic church windows,
submissive and silent.

You see me in welfare lines,
hands open wide,
waiting for what's coming to me.
Drinking death-causing concoctions
behind dumpsters.
You see me as a standing statistic,
a living, breathing, heaving stereotype.

You see me in the bar,
another joke
for you and your friends.
Just
another
squaw,
but if you want to get laid,
I'm your
Pocahontas.

You see me
as dispensable.

This is how you see me.

Undeserving of stars,
deserving of starlight rides
and pleasurable times.

Funny how you fail
to see me
when I'm
face up, lips puffed,
body bloated and battered,
bruised beyond recognition.
Still not gaining your attention.

Come on, baby,
and dance me outside.
I think she was just looking
for a good time.
I heard she lived
a risky lifestyle.
It was inevitable, some say.
This is how you see me.

Never somebody's daughter,
never somebody's mother,
never an aunt, a sister, a friend.

Never am I seen
as strong,
as proud,
as resilient.
Never as I am.

Finally, given the stars,
laid to gaze at them on back roads
and in ditches,
on ghostly stretches of
forgotten pebbled pathways.
Your vastness
swallows me.
Do I fall in your line of sight?
Do you see me now, Stephen Harper?[97]

Because I get this feeling
that your eyes,
they curve
around me.

Endnotes

INTRODUCTION

1   http://www.cbc.ca/news/canada/manitoba/harper-
    rebuffs-renewed-calls-for-murdered-missing-women-
    inquiry-1.2742845

2   http://www.cbc.ca/news/politics/full-text-of-peter-
    mansbridge's-interview-with-stephen-harper-1.2876934

3   "Missing and Murdered Indigenous Women in British
    Columbia, Canada," Inter-American Commission of
    Human Rights, Organization of American States, Decem-
    ber 21, 2014. http://www.oas.org/en/iachr/reports/pdfs/
    indigenous-women-bc-canada-en.pdf

4   "Violence against Indigenous women and girls in Canada.
    Review of reports and recommendations," Legal Strat-
    egy Coalition on Violence Against Indigenous Women,
    February 26, 2015. leaf.ca/wp-content/uploads/2015/02/
    Executive-Summary.pdf

5   "Report of the inquiry concerning Canada of the Commit-
    tee of the Elimination of Discrimination against Women
    under article 8 of the Optional Protocol to the Conven-
    tion on the Elimination of All Forms of Discrimination

against Women," United Nations, March 6, 2015. http://
tbinternet.ohchr.org/Treaties/CEDAW/Shared%20Docu-
ments/CAN/CEDAW_C_OP-8_CAN_1_7643_E.pdf

6   "Missing and Murdered Aboriginal Women: A National
    Operational Overview," Royal Canadian Mounted Police
    (RCMP), May 16, 2014. http://www.rcmp-grc.gc.ca/pubs/
    mmaw-faapd-eng.pdf

CHAPTER 3

1   "Kiskiski Awasisak: Remember the Children: Under-
    standing the Overrepresentation of First Nations Chil-
    dren in the Child Welfare System," *Information Bulletin
    CEPB #23F*, Toronto, University of Toronto, Social Work
    Faculty, 2005.

CHAPTER 4

1   Brendan Kennedy, "Without a Trace," *Ottawa Citizen*,
    September 6, 2009.

CHAPTER 5

1   Anniversary of the death of Gladys Tolley, Bridget's
    mother, the Kitigan Zibi activist and co-founder of
    Families of Sisters in Spirit. Gladys Tolley was killed by a
    Sûreté du Québec (SQ) squad car in Kitigan Zibi.

2   In 2013 and 2014, a dozen memory walks and a hundred
    Sisters in Spirit gatherings took place in Canada and else-
    where. It is a world of missing person posters, petitions,
    artists' installations, trains blocked by demonstrators,
    macabre interactive cards to which new murders and
    disappearances are added daily, documents referred to

as "tool boxes" drafted for Indigenous communities and the general public by NWAC ("Give a class presentation on the subject of missing and murdered Indigenous women and girls" or "What can I do to help the families of missing and murdered Indigenous women?").

3   Maryanne Pearce, *An Awkward Silence: Missing and Murdered Vulnerable Women and the Canadian Justice System*, University of Ottawa, Faculty of Law, 2013, p. 250, www.ruor.uottawa.ca/handle/10393/26299

4   The Oppal Commission, also responsible for an update on police failings in investigations into the Downtown Eastside's murders and disappearances.

5   "Between 1997 and 2000, the rate of homicide for Aboriginal females was 5.4 per 100,000 population, compared to 0.8 per 100,000 for non-Aboriginal victims (almost seven times higher)." *Women in Canada: A Gender-based Statistical Report*, 89-503-X, Statistics Canada, http://www.statcan.gc.ca/pub/89-503-x/2010001/article/11442-eng.htm#a35

6   "As of March 31, 2010, 582 cases of missing and murdered Aboriginal women and girls have been entered into the NWAC's Sisters in Spirit database [Editor's note: over a period of thirty years] ... More than half of the women were under the age of 31." Native Women's Association of Canada, *What Their Stories Tell Us: Research Findings of the Sisters in Spirit Initiative*, 3rd edition, March 2010.

7   Maryanne Pearce, *An Awkward Silence*. The number 912 is not the one found in the thesis, since Maryanne Pearce regularly adds names to her database.

8   In the province of Saskatchewan, 60% of missing women
     are Indigenous yet they represent only 6% of the popu-
     lation. *Provincial Partnership Committee on Missing
     Persons, Final Report,* October 2007. Cited by Amnesty
     International, *No More Stolen Sisters: The need for a com-
     prehensive response to discrimination and violence against
     Indigenous women in Canada,* 2009.

9   Author's note: 1 million out of 34 million.

10   Royal Canadian Mounted Police, *Missing and Murdered
     Aboriginal Women: A National Operational Overview,*
     May 16, 2014, www.rcmp-grc.gc.ca/pubs/mmaw-faapd-
     eng.pdf

11   Her testimonial is found in the Appendices, p. 192.

12   The Nikal cousins are missing.

13   Sources for the list: personal archive of articles and testi-
     monials gathered during vigils, provided to the *Winnipeg
     Free Press* on murders and disappearances in Manitoba,
     Maryanne Pearce, *An Awkward Silence.*

CHAPTER 6

1   Brendan Kennedy, "Without a Trace."

2   Pearce, *An Awkward Silence* (the numbers cited by
     Maryanne Pearce come from Statistics Canada studies);
     Annual Report of the Correctional Investigator of Canada,
     November 2013; Amnesty International, *No More Stolen
     Sisters* (Amnesty's numbers come from the following
     studies: Janet Smylie and Paul Adomako [editors], *Indigen-
     ous Children's Health Report: Health Assessment in Action,*
     Centre for Research on Inner City Health, 2009; *Aboriginal
     Peoples in Canada in 2006: Inuit, Métis and First Nations,*

2006 census, Statistics Canada); Jodi-Anne Brzozowski,
Andrea Taylor-Butts and Sara Johnson, "Victimization and
Offending among the Aboriginal Population in Canada,"
Juristat, vol. 26, no. 3, Canadian Centre for Justice Sta-
tistics, 2006; Vivian O'Donnell and Susan Wallace, *First
Nations, Métis and Inuit Women,* Statistics Canada.

3   Carey Marsden, "First Nations Community Calls for
Help After String of Youth Suicides," *globalnews.ca,*
April 29, 2014, www.globalnews.ca/news/1299917/first-
nations-community-calls-for-help-after-string-of-youth-
suicides

4   In 2014–15, Alana Boileau, with Annie Bergeron, an Innu
research officer, began research into the murders and
disappearances of Indigenous women in Quebec. The
resulting thesis should be made public in the fall of 2015
and serve as a foundation for the implementation of concrete measures. Among Alana and Annie's suggestions
are: a campaign to caution young girls arriving in cities
from their isolated communities who find themselves
in a situation of extreme vulnerability; the systematic
use of social media by police and social workers whenever a teenaged girl disappears; a mention of MMIW in
textbooks; an awareness campaign around non-violence
beginning at a very young age, targeting the communities; the development of protocol for reserve police
called to intervene with the families and friends of the
disappeared. In the long term, Alana and Quebec Native
Women are calling for improved living conditions for
Indigenous peoples (housing, access to employment . . .),
which are key to reducing violence against women.

5   Royal Canadian Mounted Police, *Missing and Murdered Aboriginal Women: National Operational Overview.*

6   Based on the numbers in the first RCMP report, Amnesty International calculated that Indigenous women "are 3.5 times more likely than non-Indigenous women to be murdered by a spouse or family member and 7 times more likely to be murdered by an acquaintance—this could be a friend, neighbour, colleague, or another man who is not an intimate partner of the victims—the Aboriginal identity of such acquaintances is not known." Hence, domestic violence, often cited as the principal contributor to the murders, has been overestimated. Source: "What happened at the National Roundtable on Missing and Murdered Indigenous Women and Girls?" Amnesty International, March 1, 2015. http://www. amnesty.ca/blog/what-happened-at-the-national-roundtable-on-missing-and-murdered-indigenous-women-and-girls

CHAPTER 7

1   Michèle Audette stepped down from the position of president in December 2014.

2   Leanne Simpson, "Not Murdered and Not Missing," *nationsrising.org,* March 5, 2014, www.nationsrising.org/not-murdered-and-not-missing

3   Human Rights Watch, *Those Who Take Us Away: Abusive Policing and Failures in Protection of Indigenous Women and Girls in Northern British Columbia, Canada,* February 13, 2013, www.hrw.org/report/2013/02/13/those-who-

take-us-away/abusive-policing-and-failures-protec-
tion-indigenous-women

4   Antonia Zerbisias, "Three Women, Three Deaths, One
Thing in Common," *Toronto Star*, January 2014.

5   Mike Blanchfield, "Canada Rejects UN Rights Review of
Violence Against Aboriginal Women," *Toronto Star,* September 19, 2013.

6   In 2010, funding allotted to the Sisters in Spirit program that allowed NWAC to investigate cases of missing
and murdered Indigenous women was redirected to a
national centre.

7   Melinda Maldonado, "Loretta Barbara Grace Saunders,
1987–2014," *Maclean's,* March 22, 2014, www.macleans.
ca/society/loretta-barbara-grace-saunders-1987-2014

8   Darryl Leroux, "Loretta Saunders: Courage, Strength
and Resilience," *Halifax Media Co-op,* February 20, 2014,
halifax.mediacoop.ca/story/loretta-saunders-courage-
and-strength-and-resilience/21773

9   On April 22, 2015, the two people sub-letting her apartment pled guilty to Loretta's murder. On April 28, 2015,
they were sentenced to life in prison.

10 Special Committee on Violence Against Indigenous
Women, hearing of November 21, 2013.

11 Devon Black, "A national tragedy lands in a bucket
of whitewash," *ipolitics.ca,* March 20, 2014, ipolitics.
ca/2014/03/10/a-national-tragedy-lands-in-a-bucket-of-
whitewash

12 Andrea Landry, "Why We Don't Need a Missing and Murdered Indigenous Women's Inquiry," *Last Real Indians,*

March 13, 2014, www.lastrealindians.com/why-we-dont-
need-a-missing-and-murdered-indigenous-womens-in-
quiry-by-andrea-landry

13   Helen Knott's complete poem is found in the Appendices,
      pp. 197.

CHAPTER 8

1   "A Letter From Laurie Odjick," *missingjustice.ca,* May
      2009. The full letter is found in the Appendices, p.185.

2   Brendan Kennedy, "Without a Trace."

3   Three years later, in response to a question pursuant
      to the publication of an article in *La Presse,* Quebec's
      Minister of Aboriginal Affairs, Geoffrey Kelley, acknow-
      ledged before the National Assembly that there had been
      "obviously, failings in this case . . . confusion at the begin-
      ning of the investigation." Cited in Isabelle Hachey, "Dis-
      appearance of Aboriginal Women: Kelley acknowledges
      failings," *lapresse.ca,* November 9, 2011, www.lapresse.ca/
      actualites/justice-et-affaires-criminelles/201111/09/01-
      4465935-disparition-de-femmes-autochtones-kelley-re-
      connait-des-manquements.php

4   Brendan Kennedy, "Without a Trace."

5   Ibid.

6   "A Letter From Laurie Odjick."

7   Regarding Indigenous youth in the U.S., see in particular
      Jennifer Benoit-Bryan, *National Runaway Safeline's 2013
      Reporter's Source Book on Runaway and Homeless Youth,*
      University of Illinois-Chicago, August 2013.

8   "Not Just a Video Game: The Obsessive World of Gaming
      and Its Young Stars," *CBC News,* March 6, 2009, www.cbc.

ca/news/canada/not-just-a-video-game-the-obsessive-world-of-gaming-and-its-young-stars-1.809580

9   "David Fortin's Family Keeps Hope Alive," *TVA Nouvelles*, February 10, 2013, www.tvanouvelles.ca/lcn/infos/faits divers/archives/2013/02/20130210-135314.html

10 Special Committee on Violence Against Indigenous Women, *Invisible Women: Call to Action. A Report on Missing and Murdered Indigenous Women in Canada*, House of Commons, March 2014, December 9, 2013, hearings.

11 Maryanne Pearce, *An Awkward Silence*, p. 503.

12 Numbers come from Maryanne Pearce, *An Awkward Silence*.

13 Human Rights Watch, *Those Who Take Us Away*.

14 Human Rights Watch, "Canada: Abusive Policing, Neglect Along the 'Highway of Tears'," http://www.hrw.org/news/2013/02/13/canada-abusive-policing-neglect-along-highway-tears

15 Maryanne Pearce, *An Awkward Silence*, p. 70.

CHAPTER 9

1   Kristen Gilchrist, "'Newsworthy' Victims? Exploring Differences in Canadian Local Coverage of Missing/Murdered Aboriginal and White Women," *Feminist Media Studies*, vol. 10, no. 4, 2010.

2   Quoted in Warren Goulding, *Just Another Indian: A Serial Killer and Canada's Indifference*, Calgary, Fifth House, 2001.

3   "Missing Maisy and Shannon," *Ottawa Citizen*, September 11, 2009.

CHAPTER 10

1   The Cree are the largest Indigenous group in the country.

CHAPTER 11

1   Maya Rolbin-Ghanie, "The Search for Maisy and Shannon," *The Dominion,* May 11, 2009, www.dominionpaper.ca/weblogs/%5Buser%5D/2650

CHAPTER 12

1   Maryanne Pearce, *An Awkward Silence.*
2   Ibid., p. 3.

CHAPTER 13

1   Kim Dramer, *The Chipewyan (Indians of North America),* New York, Chelsea House Publishers, 1996.
2   Sylvia van Kirk revolutionized the view of the fur trade by describing the pre-eminent role of Indigenous women (*Many Tender Ties,* Winnipeg, Watson & Dwyer, 1980).
3   John Demos, *The Tried and the True: Native American Women Confronting Colonization,* New York, Oxford University Press, 1995.
4   Ibid.
5   Before it became plagued with social and environmental problems, Fort Chipewyan embodied a thriving multicultural, egalitarian society thanks to the fur trade. See "A World We Have Lost: The Plural Society of Fort Chipewyan," in Robin Jarvis Brownlie and Valerie J. Korinek, *Finding a Way to the Heart: Feminist Writings on Aboriginal Women's History in Canada,* Winnipeg, University of Manitoba Press, 2012.
6   The conversation can be accessed at www.kare.ca
7   Marie-France Labrecque, *De Ciudad Juárez à l'autoroute*

des larmes, ces femmes autochtones que l'on tue en toute impunité, Montreal, Cahiers DIALOG, INRS, 2014.

8 *Statistics Canada. Aboriginal statistics at a glance (21 June, 2010)* Ottawa: Statistics Canada, 2007.

9 *Statistics Canada. Remaining life expectancy at age 25 and probability of survival to age 75, by socioeconomic status and Aboriginal ancestry,* by Michael Tjepkema and Russell Wilkins (4 December, 2011), p. 1.

10 Emma Larocque, written submission for "Aboriginal Justice Inquiry Hearings," 1990, cited in the study *Marginalized: The Aboriginal Women's Experience in Federal Corrections,* Public Safety Canada, http://www.publicsafety. gc.ca/cnt/rsrcs/pblctns/mrgnlzd/index-eng.aspx

11 Indigenous peoples' attachment to their Indian status might seem surprising since it is reminiscent of segregation or apartheid. *"But the reserves also allow for the survival of the First Nations identity, deemed by many Indigenous peoples as more important than belonging to Canada."*

12 Amnesty International, *Canada: Stolen Sisters: A Human Rights Response to Discrimination and Violence Against Indigenous Women in Canada,* 2004. amnesty.ca/sites/ default/files/amr200032004enstolensisters.pdf

13 Regarding this issue, read pages 167–70 in Thomas King's *The Inconvenient Indian: A Curious Account of Native People in North America,* Toronto, Doubleday Canada, 2012.

CHAPTER 14

1 Josiane Loiselle-Bourdeau, Health Coordinator, Quebec

Native Women (QNW), and Wanda Gabriel, social support worker in the Mohawk community of Kanesatake.

2 There are eleven Innu nations in Quebec in the North Shore and Saguenay–Lac-Saint-Jean regions.

3 Naomi Fontaine, *Kuessipan,* Montreal, Mémoire d'encrier, 2011, pp. 27–28 in French.

4 Aboriginal Psychosocial Interventions Research Group, Étude sur l'abus sexuel chez les Premières Nations du Québec (Study on Sexual Abuse Among Quebec's First Nations), March 2005.

5 Cherry Kingsley and Melanie Mark, *Sacred Lives: Canadian Aboriginal Children & Youth Speak Out About Sexual Exploitation,* National Aboriginal Consultation Project, 2000.

6 "Domestic Sex Trafficking of Aboriginal Girls in Canada: Issues and Implications," *First Peoples Child & Family Review* 3, no. 3 (2007), First Nations Caring Society of Canada, 2007.

7 Annette Sikka, *Trafficking of Aboriginal Women and Girls in Canada.*

8 Anupriya Sethi, "Domestic Sex Trafficking of Aboriginal Girls in Canada," note 6.

9 Annette Sikka, *Trafficking of Aboriginal Women and Girls in Canada.*

10 Ibid.

11 Cherry Kingsley and Melanie Mark, *Sacred Lives,* note 5.

CHAPTER 15

1 The Tribal Council for the Algonquin Anishinabe nation

in Kitigan Zibi encompasses six of Quebec's Algonquin
communities.

2   In *Since Time Immemorial: Our Story,* Stephen
McGregor's book on the history of Kitigan Zibi, the
author explains that "Kitigan Zibi" is not a translation of
"Desert River," but of "River of Gardens." The two names
may seem contradictory, but the name "Desert River"
comes from the fact that there were few trees on the
plain surrounding the river, the future site for the reserve.

3   "The contribution of genetic data to the genealogical
measurement of French-Canadians' Indigenous origins,"
Cahiers québécois de démographie, vol. 41, spring 2012.

4   This incomplete list comes from Maryanne Pearce's thesis.
Locations and details come from personal investigation.

5   Royal Canadian Mounted Police, *Missing and Murdered
Aboriginal Women: National Operational Overview.*

6   Namely, the Sept-Îles, Pointe-Bleue, La Tuque and Amos
residential schools as well as Fort George's two residential schools. *Directory of Residential Schools in Canada,*
Aboriginal Healing Foundation, Ottawa, 2007.

7   This poor, isolated community is located 175 km northwest of Maniwaki in the Parc de la Vérendrye. Some
Barrier Lake young people board in Maniwaki while
attending school.

CHAPTER 16

1   "Missing Maisy and Shannon," *Ottawa Citizen,* September 11, 2009.

2   See chapter 8.

3   I have deleted the name of the gang. First names and
     initials have been changed.

CONNIE GREYEYES' SPEECH ON PARLIAMENT HILL

4   Stephen Harper's name was added to the original text by
     Connie Greyeyes with Helen Knott's permission.

LIST OF REPORTS CONSULTED

(Chronological order, based on publication date 2000–15)

Cherry Kingsley and Melanie Mark, *Sacred Lives: Canadian Aboriginal Children & Youth Speak Out About Sexual Exploitation,* National Aboriginal Consultation Project, 2000.

Amnesty International, *Canada: Stolen Sisters: A Human Rights Response to Discrimination and Violence against Indigenous Women in Canada,* October 2004.

Jodi-Anne Brzozowski, Andrea Taylor-Butts and Sara Johnson, "Victimization and offending among the Aboriginal population in Canada," *Juristat,* vol. 26, no. 3, Canadian Centre for Justice Statistics, 2006.

Anupriya Sethi, "Domestic Sex Trafficking of Aboriginal Girls in Canada: Issues and Implications," *First Peoples Child & Family Review,* vol. 3, no. 3 (2007), First Nations Caring Society of Canada, 2007.

Quebec Native Women, *Les femmes autochtones et la violence,* Report presented to Dr. Yakin Ertürk, UN Special Rapporteur on Violence Against Women, January 2008.

Native Women's Association of Canada, *Voices of Our Sisters in Spirit: A Report to Families and Communities,* November 2008 and March 2009.

Amnesty International, *No More Stolen Sisters: The need for a comprehensive response to discrimination and violence against Indigenous women in Canada,* 2009.

Shannon Brennan, *Violent victimization of Aboriginal women in the Canadian provinces,* Statistics Canada, 2009.

Anette Sikka, *Trafficking of Aboriginal Women and Girls in Canada,* University of Ottawa, Institute on Governance, 2009.

Native Women's Association of Canada, "Root Causes of Violence Against Aboriginal Women and the Impact of Colonization," in *Community Resource Guide: What Can I Do to Help the Families of Missing and Murdered Aboriginal Women and Girls?* 2010.

Native Women's Association of Canada, *What Their Stories Tell Us: Research Findings from the Sisters in Spirit Initiative,* 3rd edition, March 2010.

Kristen Gilchrist, "'Newsworthy' Victims? Exploring Differences in Canadian Local Coverage of Missing/Murdered Aboriginal and White Women," *Feminist Media Studies,* vol. 10, no. 4, 2010.

Standing Committee on the Status of Women, *Call into the Night: An Overview of Violence Against Aboriginal Women,* Interim Report, House of Commons, March 2011.

Standing Committee on the Status of Women, *Ending Violence Against Aboriginal Women and Girls: Empowerment—A New Beginning,* Final Report, House of Commons, December 2011.

Lyse Montminy et al., *La violence conjugale et les femmes autochtones au Québec: état des lieux et des interventions,* Preliminary Report presented to the Fonds de recherche québécois sur la société et la culture, within the framework of a joint action plan, 2011.

Wally T. Oppal, *Forsaken,* Report of the Missing Women Commission of Inquiry, November 2012.

Human Rights Watch, *Those Who Take Us Away. Abusive Policing and Failures in Protection of Indigenous Women and Girls in Northern British Columbia, Canada,* February 13, 2013.

Maryanne Pearce, *An Awkward Silence: Missing and Murdered Vulnerable Women and the Canadian Justice System,* University of Ottawa, Faculty of Law, 2013.

Special Committee on Violence Against Indigenous Women, *Invisible Women: A Call to Action. A Report on Missing and Murdered Indigenous Women in Canada,* House of Commons, March 2014.

Royal Canadian Mounted Police, *Missing and Murdered Aboriginal Women: National Operational Overview,* May 2014.

Inter-American Commission of Human Rights, Organization of American States, "Missing and Murdered Indigenous Women in British Columbia, Canada," December 21, 2014.

Legal Strategy Coalition on Violence Against Indigenous Women, "Violence against Indigenous women and girls in Canada. Review of reports and recommendations," February 26, 2015.

Amnesty International, "What happened at the National Roundtable on Missing and Murdered Indigenous Women and Girls?" March 1, 2015.

United Nations, "Report of the inquiry concerning Canada of the Committee of the Elimination of Discrimination against Women under article 8 of the Optional Protocol to the Convention on the Elimination of All Forms of Discrimination against Women," March 6, 2015.